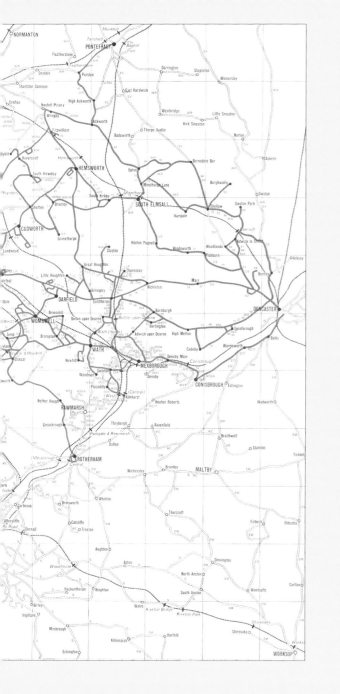

EXPRESS

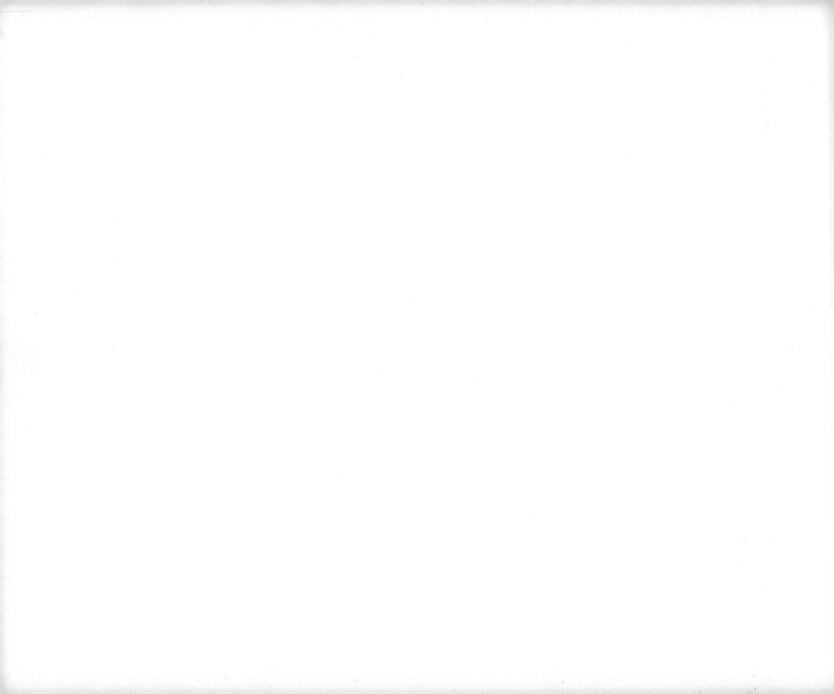

Yorkshire Traction

GLORY
DAYS

BIRMINGHAM EXPRESS

Yorkshire Traction

233

LEOPARD

UHE 233H

Bob Telfer

Ian Allan
PUBLISHING

Contents

Foreword …	… … … … … …	3
Introduction	… … … … … …	4
1.	Barnsley & District … … … …	6
2.	Yorkshire Traction before the war… … … …	10
3.	War and peace … … … … …	17
4.	The 1950s … … … … … … …	27
5.	The final years of BET … … … … …	52
6.	County Motors … … … … … …	62
7.	Mexborough & Swinton … … … … …	66
8.	NBC — the early years … … … … …	71
9.	NBC — the corporate image … … … …	78
10.	Independence … … … … … …	85
11.	Barnsley & District revived … ……… …	92
12.	Stagecoach … … … … … …	94
Bibliography	… … … … … … …	96

First published 2008

ISBN 978 0 7110 3226 2

Published by Ian Allan Publishing an imprint of Ian Allan Publishing Ltd, Hersham, Surrey, KT12 4RG

Printed in England by Ian Allan Printing Ltd, Hersham, Surrey, KT12 4RG

Code: 0806/B

Visit the Ian Allan Publishing website at www.ianallanpublishing.com

Foreword

One of my earliest memories is of Saturday morning, standing waiting for the 9.25 bus into Barnsley. The bright red single-decker would turn up and we would clamber up the steep and awkward stairs. The conductor (or sometimes conductress) would hold open a heavy-looking door and we would take our seats, my mother asking for a nine-penny and a five-penny ticket — our passports to a morning's shopping.

A few years later, queues of Leyland Tiger Cubs parked outside the working men's club, ready to take us off to Blackpool, Scarborough or Skegness on the annual club trip. Wooden cases of bottles of pop and a pound note to spend at the end of the journey to the sea.

Later still, the first day at senior school and a four-mile bus ride, this time on the 65 towards Sheffield, a route immortalised by Barry Hines in his novel *The Blinder*. And back home at four o'clock — a fearsome rugby scrum at the bus stop because there were never enough seats and the 20-minute wait for the number 67 was far too long to contemplate.

My first day at work began with a Yorkshire Traction bus ride. Then there were more bus rides for evenings out — and days out, to Finningley Air Show, for example. Standing in Barnsley bus station, wondering about some of those exotic destinations — how could Grimethorpe have both a White City and a Red City? Just how did a Yorkshire Traction bus get to California? And for sheer comedy value you can't beat being able to say: "This bus is going to Jump" (and, if it was a number 25, it certainly would be).

Yorkshire Traction was a central part of my life for the first 18 years or so. Then — like so many others — I learned to drive. Work demanded that I *should* drive rather than catch a bus. But I still sneaked back for a bus ride on odd days off. I was privileged to be there when Yorkshire Traction celebrated its 85th birthday, and I was as sorry as anyone to learn that the company's talent for survival in a post-deregulation and post-privatisation world had finally deserted it and that it was to become an anonymous part of a major transport group.

For a company that never really wanted to run buses — it was started as a tram company — the 'Tracky', as it will always be known to me and many thousands of others, didn't do a bad job. In many ways it served its communities well, and it is a joy to see so many of its memories preserved in this volume.

Alan Whitehouse
BBC Yorkshire Transport Correspondent

This bus isn't going to jump. It isn't even going to Jump, whatever it might say on the front. Guy Arab 685 (NCX 176) had just been taken over from County Motors and found itself in very unfamiliar territory, operating an extended journey on service 22 from Barnsley to Doncaster via Mexborough and on to the annual Finningley Air Display. RAF Finningley was well away from normal Tracky territory and was served mainly by the local independent operator, Leon Motor Services. Here 685 is negotiating the roundabout outside Doncaster South bus station, usual terminus of the 22. *Roger Holmes*

Introduction

Yorkshire Traction was one of the best-known names in the business for nearly 80 years and, together with its predecessor Barnsley & District, was part of daily life in the south-western corner of Yorkshire for more than a century. Invariably known as 'Tracky', the company was respected locally and nationally.

Now — with the name so recently disappeared from the public eye — is the perfect time to look back at past glories. However, there is no room for sentimentality; this was no rags-to-riches tale of a small local business but a hard-nosed enterprise established (in 1902) by one of Britain's biggest commercial empires, with the purse-strings firmly held in London. It was a roller-coaster ride, with partial nationalisation in 1948, full state-ownership from 1968 and privatisation in 1987. In local ownership the going was tough, and it came as no great surprise when Tracky fell to the multinational Stagecoach group in late 2005.

There was nothing intrinsically remarkable about Tracky buses; until the 1970s most were typical of the British Electric Traction group, and the majority came from Leyland, Britain's biggest and best-known bus builder. They were worked hard, and functionality was the key requirement. Buses from acquired operators added variety, and many ran for a time in Tracky livery; it has even been said that Norman Dean, Tracky's longest-serving and most popular General Manager, liked a few quirky vehicles 'to keep the engineers on their toes'!

Although centred on Barnsley, Tracky's bus services radiated out to the West Riding's three great cities, Bradford, Leeds and Sheffield, and stretched eastwards to Doncaster and west to Huddersfield and Holmfirth, with tentacles across the Pennines to Manchester. Barnsley was built on coal, and the coalfield stretched from the west of the town through the Dearne Valley towards Doncaster; to the north the woollen and textile trades dominated, while to the south lay the heart of the country's iron and steel industry.

Tracky's landscape could be grim, yet there were many rural services, running through attractive and sometimes wild countryside and dozens of delightful villages. In their red and cream livery the buses blended well with their environment, whether it was the pitheads and spoil heaps of the coalfield,

the high moorland of the Pennine fringes around Holmfirth and Penistone or the urban centres, where they rubbed shoulders with the municipal buses, trams and trolleybuses of Bradford, Doncaster, Halifax, Huddersfield, Leeds, Rotherham, Sheffield and, on the famous trans-Pennine services, also with those of Manchester, Ashton-under-Lyne and others.

Tracky also ran coaches. From the start of the 1930s express services took them daily to Birmingham and London as well as to Blackpool and Scarborough, gaining almost national recognition, while private hires catered for mass outings organised by the miners' welfare clubs. This contrast is part of the fascination.

This is not a comprehensive history of Tracky but a nostalgic look at the company over the years, in the context of the areas and the people it served. It focuses on the 'glory days', which in this series of books are for the author to define. This was no easy task, but I settled on the period from 1935 to 1972. Why? Because 1935 marked the transition from an era of rapid expansion into one of stability and prosperity, while 1972 marked the end of an era, with the arrival of the last vehicles in traditional livery. It is no coincidence that for two-thirds of this time Norman Dean was at the helm. To set the scene I have also covered the years before and after — the rise and fall — both periods being rather more complex than the stable 'glory days'.

My personal recollections cover only the end of the 'glory days', as a teenager visiting grandparents in Yorkshire, when our usual transport was a coach — often a Tracky coach — on the 'Ten Cities Express'. Buses had fascinated me from an early age, but I gave little thought to who ran them or how they were run. Nevertheless, I became drawn in, and one day in the early 1980s a vacancy notice appeared in the Middlesbrough office of United Automobile Services, where I then worked, seeking a Chief Traffic Officer for Yorkshire Traction (with hindsight this sounds rather grand — it wasn't!). On the strength of that I arrived in Barnsley and worked for Tracky for six eventful years before moving on.

In working on this book I have been fortunate to have the willing and generous help of many people — archivists, colleagues, enthusiasts, historians and above all the photographers

Yorkshire winters aren't what they used to be! Here a Leyland Tiger, possibly on service 27 to Rotherham, battles along Upper Sheffield Road past Barsnley depot in the wake of a heavy snowfall in February 1940. This was (and still is) the main A61, which then ran from Thirsk to Derby via Harrogate, Leeds, Wakefield, Barnsley, Sheffield and Chesterfield. The scene is little different today, except that modern street lighting has replaced the telegraph poles.
Barnsley Archives and Local Studies

who recorded Tracky's day-to-day activities in the days when high-quality photography was much more difficult than it is now. Their assistance is gratefully acknowledged, and it is almost entirely their efforts which will have made this book a success. All photographs are credited where the photographer or the source is known, but I apologise now for any omissions or errors; it has not been possible to identify the source of every photograph, and some have cropped up more than once from different sources.

Singling out individuals is an invidious task, but amongst the many people to whom I am indebted the following deserve a special mention: H. John Black, Michael Fowler, John Fozard, Roger Holmes, Bruce Jenkins, John Kaye, John Law, Iain MacGregor, Peter Roberts, Colin Routh, Richard Simons and Tony Wilson, for going out of the way to help with their own photographic material; Alan Whitehouse, for contributing the Foreword; Alistair Douglas, Mike Eyre, Martin Jenkins and Charles Roberts of the Online Transport Archive and Mike Sutcliffe, for making other photographers' work available; Jim Sykes (my predecessor at Tracky), for placing on record the findings of his superbly detailed research into the company's early history; and Alan Townsin, for solving some mysteries in connection with the prewar fleet. In addition I am grateful to the volunteer officers of the Omnibus Society, the PSV Circle and the Kithead Trust and to the staff at Barnsley Archives and, last but not least, to all at Ian Allan Publishing.

I have enjoyed compiling this trip back in time, and I hope you enjoy the results.

Bob Telfer
Sheffield
January 2008

1. Barnsley & District

For its first 10 years the Barnsley & District Electric Traction Co was exclusively a tramway operator, not diversifying into motor buses until 1913. In this busy scene at the terminus in Worsbrough Dale High Street, 1902 car No 6 has just operated out from Barnsley along Sheffield Road and descended the steep single-track line along the High Street from the Cutting Edge. These cars had been built with open top decks but were soon enclosed in a fairly crude manner, as shown here. This stretch of road remains quite recognisable today. *Author's collection; source unknown*

The Barnsley & District Electric Traction Co was incorporated in March 1902 as a subsidiary of British Electric Traction, the country's foremost tramway operator. Electric tramways were springing up throughout the country in the first decade of the century, and every self-respecting borough wanted one, whether run by private enterprise or by the municipal authorities. By 1910 the West Riding of Yorkshire could boast around a dozen.

Barnsley's tramway opened in November 1902 and extended for about three miles. From its northern terminus by the gasworks on Old Mill Lane at Smithies, just short of the bridge over the Barnsley Coal Railway, the line climbed steeply up Eldon Street North to the town centre, continuing along Sheffield Road and then splitting to serve termini at Worsbrough Bridge and Worsbrough Dale.

A depot was built on land on Upper Sheffield Road, about half a mile south of the town centre, and this was still the hub of Yorkshire Traction's operations a century later.

Twelve open-top double-deck cars were supplied by Brush of Loughborough and were soon equipped with basic top covers, then quite a rarity. Custom on the Smithies section proved disappointing, so from 1905 this was run with a small one-man car, the double-deckers working mainly the Sheffield Road services. Another double-decker came in 1912, but in 1914 one of the original cars was scrapped after careering down Eldon Street North, so the fleet was back to 13.

The trams were not as profitable as BET had hoped, and plans to extend the system were dropped. However, by 1910 the potential of the motor bus was clear, and the local manager, Paul Henri di Marco, won the support of the BET board to bring motor buses to Barnsley. In 1912 land adjoining the tram sheds was acquired for a bus garage. Five Brush-bodied Leyland 'S' types were obtained, with some of the earliest County Borough of Barnsley registrations (HE 8-12), and services to Goldthorpe, Grimethorpe, Hoyland, Royston and West Melton started in May 1913. The response was overwhelming, almost 20,000 passengers being carried in the first three weeks.

Within a year B&D had 20 similar buses, and services reached as far as Doncaster and Pontefract, but the war stopped expansion and forced service reductions, despite official recognition of the company's role in transporting miners. Eight buses went to help maintain BET's Peterborough and Reading operations and others were commandeered. Many staff enlisted, including Mr di Marco himself, and in 1915 Walter Nicoll became General Manager. 'Girl conductors' were also taken on. Timetables varied according to the availability of staff, petrol and spare parts, but Nicoll was credited with doing a remarkable job in keeping services going.

As stopgap measures at least one bus was converted to run on coal gas, with a huge fabric bag on its roof, and a Thornycroft chassis was acquired and fitted with a second-hand bus body.

After the war Nicoll was eager to expand B&D's bus operations, and to reflect this 'Electric' was deleted from the company title. All investment now went into buses; more Leylands were ordered, and new or improved services began as fast as they arrived. Between 1919 and 1924 ninety were added to stock, including six acquired from BET's Gateshead-based subsidiary, Northern General. Some probably used reconditioned ex-military chassis, while later examples were of Leyland's rather ungainly 'side-type', with the driver squeezed alongside the engine instead of sitting behind it, maximising passenger space. Bodies were by Brush or Strachan & Brown and painted maroon (early buses had carried BET's two-tone green, as on Mike Sutcliffe's immaculately restored 1913 S type, HE 12), this livery later evolving into 'traditional' Yorkshire Traction red and cream.

In 1920 the trams still carried more passengers than the buses, but nine years later journeys by tram had dipped below two million, while bus journeys had soared to over 20 million.

Services extended westwards to Penistone and Huddersfield by 1923, and another ran to Thurnscoe via Wath, following the route of the Dearne District Light Railways, a municipally owned folly which opened in 1924.

Many men had cut their teeth on motor vehicles during war service and were ideal recruits to B&D's ranks. Others were budding entrepreneurs and, with vehicles plentiful and licences neither too difficult to get nor to avoid, set up on their own; by the mid-1920s B&D faced competition from scores of small operators. The licensing system was a mess; it functioned at council level, and in those days there were a lot of councils — the six-mile run from Barnsley to Ryhill traversed five authority areas! Whilst some were strict, others chose not to exercise their licensing powers at all (Barnsley was considered lenient, resulting in 'ramshackle conveyances driven by youths', to quote a contemporary press report. There were frequent court cases relating to unlicensed buses, but the small fines failed to deter repeat offences) Many competitors used 14-seaters, and in an attempt to counter them B&D took 20 Leyland Z7s with Ransomes 20-seat bodies for 1925, bringing fleet numbers up to 130.

Few communities were now without a bus service, and the bigger operators set out to define and protect their territories. Already B&D had agreed boundaries with BET's Yorkshire (Woollen District) Electric Tramways Co and the independent

PART OF THE COMPANY'S FLEET OF 50 MOTOR COACHES.

TIME TABLE.

BARNSLEY (ELDON ST.) & DONCASTER (WATERDALE)

Via Wombwell, Wath, Mexboro', Denaby, & Conisboro'.

WEEK-DAYS AND SUNDAYS.

S O—Saturdays only.

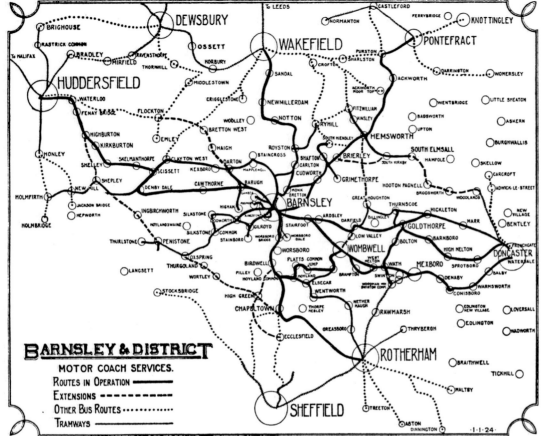

To continue expanding B&D now had to buy out other operators, and between 1925 and 1928 eight were acquired, starting in the Huddersfield area with Frank Harburn's service to Barnsley. Tom Mitchell of Kirkburton followed, his Waterloo garage briefly becoming B&D's Huddersfield base until premises in Lincoln Street were acquired in 1926. Relationships with the municipal operators were generally good, and some smaller concerns were acquired jointly. G. T. Glossop was one, selling his Sheffield–Barnsley services to Sheffield Corporation in 1926, when two buses and a share of the operation transferred to B&D. B&D then bought Hinton Bros' Barnsley–Wentworth–Rotherham service, passing three buses and half the operation to Rotherham Corporation. Further west, Huddersfield Corporation wanted to expand outside its boundary but lacked the necessary powers, so B&D acquired Ernest Sellars' Farnley Tyas service and ran it until the Corporation could take over in 1928. These deals put paid to B&D's rigid standardisation on Leylands, and Harburn's seven buses (which became B&D 131-7) included a Berliet, a Gotfredson and three Karriers, while Glossop and Hinton contributed AECs and Guys.

In 1925 Leyland Motors introduced its first bespoke passenger chassis, featuring pneumatic tyres, and encouraged B&D to evaluate a Brush-bodied Lion PLSC1. It performed well and was bought, and by the autumn of 1926 another 20 were in service. These were 30-seaters, four of them bodied by Hall Lewis (a new supplier), the rest by Brush.

Four operators were taken over in 1927, but only an ADC and an AEC from Aston of Jump were retained. This was a difficult year, the local economy being severely depressed, and for the first time since 1918 there were no new buses, the only other additions being a nearly new Lion which Yorkshire Woollen had inherited from a smaller operator, and a Leyland 'N' which had previously run as a van.

Confidence soon returned, and 40 long-wheelbase PLSC3 Lions were ordered for 1928. Thirty had 30-seat centre-entrance bodies by Brush, but the other 10 had Leyland's own 35-seat forward-entrance bodywork — the highest-capacity buses in the fleet.

B&D's largest acquisition was also the last — James Guest of

West Riding Automobile Co (causing B&D's Knottingley service to be cut back to Pontefract). To the south and east B&D's ambitions were constrained by the municipal transport systems in Sheffield, Rotherham and Doncaster, while the Mexborough & Swinton tramway monopolised the corridor north of Rotherham to Swinton and Conisbrough. To the west the Pennines formed a natural boundary which few buses then crossed, while between the Pennines and the 'heavy woollen' towns Huddersfield had a growing municipal operation. The shape of the Yorkshire Traction network of 40 years later was already recognisable.

FARES.

ROTHERHAM, via Chapeltown.

Barnsley	Worsbro' Bridge' (Police Station)								
sbro' Bridge (Police Station)	5d.	3d.	Birdwell (Excelsior Terrace)						
dwell (Obelisk	7	5	2d.	Hoyland Common (Cross Keys)					
yland Common (Allott's Corner)	9	7	4	2d.	Wentworth & Hoyland (Rly. Station)				
entworth (Harley Road)	10	8	5	3	2d.	Chapeltown (Norfolk Arms)			
apeltown (Norfolk Arms)	1/-	10	7	5	3	2d.	Chapeltown (Waggon & Horses)		
(Waggon & Horses)........	1/2	1/-	9	7	5	4	2d.	Thorpe Common (Ball Inn)	
orpe Common (Ball Inn)	1/3	1/1	10	8	6	5	3	2d.	Lodge Lane
dge Lane	1/4	1/2	1/-	10	8	6	5	4	3½d. Dropping Well (Effingham Arms)
opping Well (Effingham Arms)..........	1/4	1/2	1/-	10	8	6	6½	5½
otherham (Bridgegate)	1/6	1/4	1/2	1/-	10	8	7	6	6½	5½

REDUCED FARES FOR CHILDREN.

If not exceeding 3-feet in height, and not occupying a seat, Free.

If not exceeding 4-ft. 6-ins. in height Half Adult Fare plus fractions of 1d., with a minimum fare of 2d.

Children travelling to or from School between 8·0 a.m. and 6·0 p.m., Mondays to Fridays inclusive, Half Adult Fare plus fractions of a 1d., with a minimum fare of 2d.

Rates for Conveyance of Luggage, Goods, Parcels, etc.

By OMNIBUS ONLY.

	A. When accompanied by passengers.	B. Unaccompanied by passengers, including free delivery up to half-a-mile from nearest Agency.
Not exceeding 14-lbs. in weight ..	Free.	5d.
" 28-lbs. " ..	Half Adult Fare	6d.
" 56-lbs. " ..	plus fractions	9d.
Dogs	of 1d.	Not carried.
Folding Mail Carts	Min. 2d. Max. 6d.	6d.

Conductors are authorised to refuse to convey parcels of a dangerous, objectionable or too bulky a nature upon the Company's vehicles.

ALL PARCELS ARE CARRIED ONLY AT OWNERS' RISK.

Parcel Agent—Mr. H. E. HOUGHTON, Tobacconist, near Gaol Bridge.

Swinton, in October 1928. Guest's 'Blue Bus Services' included routes from Mexborough to Doncaster and Kilnhurst and from Doncaster to Rotherham, which the two corporations partly replaced. Rotherham took three of Guest's 14 buses, leaving B&D with four Leylands and seven REOs. In the meantime George Robinson was appointed General Manager, following Walter Nicoll's death in March 1928, and ownership of the company transferred from BET to the newly formed TBAT (Tilling & British Automobile Traction Co).

Operations now extended well beyond Barnsley, additional depots having been established in Doncaster, Huddersfield and Mexborough, and there was a desire that this should be reflected in the company's title. Many bus operators chose geographical names, but 'South Yorkshire', 'West Riding' and 'West Yorkshire' were already spoken for, while Yorkshire Woollen buses simply sported the fleetname 'Yorkshire'. After some deliberation 'Yorkshire Traction' was chosen, and the new title was announced in December 1928, after which the Barnsley & District name quickly disappeared.

Initially coming on loan from Leyland Motors in 1925 with a 30-seat Brush body, HE 2718 was the first of Barnsley & District's many Leyland Lions. Early in 1926 it was bought and numbered 138, but in 1929 it was rebodied by Leyland and renumbered 265. This photograph, taken outside the offices at Upper Sheffield Road, with tram tracks running through the wet cobblestones in the foreground, is believed to show it in original form. Its proportions look rather odd, the wheels seeming overly large. *Author's collection; source unknown*

Under the Yorkshire Traction title business continued as before: more expansion, more takeovers, more Leylands. The starting fleet included 64 Lions, a similar number of older Leylands bought new by B&D, a few second-hand vehicles and 13 tramcars. A brighter red livery was introduced, with grey and yellow relief, and 'Traction' was used briefly as the fleetname before 'Yorkshire Traction' was settled upon.

The first full year, 1929, was an eventful one. The first regular express services started in time for the Whitsuntide holiday, leaving Barnsley for the Lancashire, Lincolnshire and Yorkshire coasts at 7am. Fares were 10s return to Blackpool or Scarborough and 9s to Cleethorpes.

Also introduced in May was an hourly bus service across the Pennines to Manchester, running alternately via Penistone and Woodhead or Holmfirth and the 'Isle of Skye', an isolated hostelry almost 1,500ft above sea level at Wessenden Head. Run jointly with the associated North Western Road Car Co, the service was arduous at the best of times but especially in winter.

Another new direction took 'Traction' buses from Doncaster through Thorne and across the flat peat moors to the port of Goole, where it was possible to change onto East Yorkshire Motor Services' Hull service, through fares being available. Uptake was disappointing, the original hourly frequency later being halved, and following the enforced withdrawal of the service in 1933 Tracky would never return to this area.

Closer to home, two Dearne Valley operators were taken over. Deverew of Thurnscoe and Stewardson of Goldthorpe both ran to Doncaster, while Stewardson also had a Barnsley service. Eleven buses were acquired, Deverew's Lion and Tiger lasting until 1936.

New buses included 40 Brush-bodied 'Long Lions', used both for expansion and to replace the last RAF-type Leylands and some of the side-types and Z7s. The coastal expresses and the Manchester services demanded something with a bit more 'go', so six six-cylinder Tiger TS2s with comfortable 26-seat Hall Lewis bodies were ordered — the first of more than 300 Tigers bought by 1950.

As express services started to develop so too did the terminology, and only now did the word 'coach' assume its modern meaning; B&D had always referred to its local bus routes as 'motor *coach*' services, whereas the Tiger coaches were 'new saloon *buses*'. Yorkshire Traction perpetuated this increasingly quaint usage well into the 1930s.

At the end of 1929 a 49% shareholding passed to the London, Midland & Scottish and London & North Eastern railway companies, giving them representation on the board of Yorkshire

At times the company portrayed itself almost with municipal pride, and a 'souvenir guide' enterprisingly produced in 1930 suggested that Barnsley without Tracky would be 'like a human being without a nervous system'!

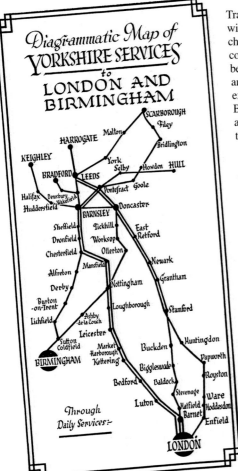

SCARBOROUGH
Filey
HARROGATE Malton
Bridlington
KEIGHLEY
York
Selby Howden HULL
BRADFORD LEEDS
Halifax Dewsbury Pontefract Goole
Huddersfield Wakefield
BARNSLEY Doncaster
Sheffield Tickhill
Dronfield Worksop East
Chesterfield Ollerton Retford
Alfreton Mansfield Newark
Derby Nottingham Grantham
Burton
-on-Trent Loughborough Stamford
Lichfield Ashby
de-la-Zouch Huntingdon
Leicester
Sutton Market Buckden
Coldfield Harborough Papworth
BIRMINGHAM Kettering Biggleswade Royston
Bedford Baldock
Stevenage Ware
Luton Hatfield Hoddesdon
Barnet
Enfield

Through Daily Services:-

LONDON

Traction, which now proclaimed itself to be 'associated with the LNE and LMS railways'. In practice little changed. The relationship was described as a 'most cordial partnership' but did not actually achieve much beyond mutual assistance in the event of breakdowns and limited inter-availability of tickets, the major exception being the provision of land for the new Barnsley bus station in the late 1930s. The UK's apparent inability to achieve an integrated public transport system goes back a long way!

The following year was no less eventful. In July 1930 Tracky's involvement in express-service operation expanded dramatically when it and Yorkshire Woollen joined the West Yorkshire Road Car Co in operating the 'Yorkshire Services' from Harrogate and Keighley to London and Birmingham. Tracky bought six Brush-bodied Tiger TS2 coaches for this work, to be supported as necessary by less-luxurious vehicles. Six Weymann-bodied TS4s followed in 1932. East Yorkshire joined in later, and Barnsley became a major interchange point, with coaches converging from Bradford, Harrogate, Hull and Keighley before heading south.

On 31 August the tramway closed after 28 years, ending Yorkshire Traction's short and often forgotten career as a tram operator. The event passed with little ceremony. The replacements were Tracky's first double-deck buses, Leyland Titan TD1s with Leyland's own side-gangway bodywork, working services 56 (Worsbrough Bridge) and 57 (Worsbrough Dale).

Leyland was now offering an improved Lion, and Tracky took 34 LT1s with Brush bodies in 1930 and 18 all-Leyland LT2s in 1931, the latter having forward entrances rather than the centre-entrance layout preferred for some years. Six further all-Leyland TD1s delivered in 1931 brought the double-deck fleet to 18.

During this period the important joint services to Bradford and Leeds were developed. Journeys from Sheffield to Barnsley were extended to Dewsbury in 1929, and to Wakefiled and Leeds in 1930, finally reaching Bradford from Dewsbury in 1932. The Bradford service was shared with Yorkshire Woollen and the

Leeds service with West Riding, while the Sheffield Joint Omnibus Committee, a collaboration of Sheffield Corporation and the LMS and LNER, would later have a share in both. Another joint SJOC/Yorkshire Traction operation was service 68 (Sheffield–Penistone–Huddersfield), which had started in B&D days, in 1928.

Of six takeovers in 1930/1 only two involved vehicles. Hollinshead & Stannard, of Bolton-on-Dearne, had operated between Goldthorpe and Mexborough and brought two ADCs and an almost-new Lion, while Arthur Walshaw's Barnsley–Millhouse Green service brought a GMC and three Karriers, as well as ending competition on the Penistone routes.

In the 1920s many small operators showed little regard for timetables, but the licensing system introduced by the 1930 Road Traffic Act changed this. The Traffic Commissioners appointed to manage the new regime had to establish who had the most legitimate claim to the licence for any contested service, and whilst most of Yorkshire Traction's applications were straightforward, matters became more complex where other operators were involved; it was a successful appeal against the decision to license Tracky's Goole service that forced its withdrawal in 1933.

The new licensing system encouraged consolidation and gave potential buyers confidence that, if they acquired a competitor, another wouldn't suddenly appear in its place. As a result, Tracky bought out four operators providing the 'XL' service to Cudworth in 1932, following these in 1933/4 with four Royston-based operators running between Barnsley and Ryhill. Thomas Wombwell was the biggest of the Royston operators, with five buses and a garage on Church Hill, which Tracky kept for many years despite its proximity to other depots and the fact that it could accommodate only three vehicles under cover. Other acquired operators were John Hellewell of Ardsley, who served Kendray and Stairfoot with a Leyland Lion and a Cub, and Albert Bentley of Smithies, who ran to Carlton and Ryhill and sold out in 1934 with five vehicles.

Until now Tracky's allegiance to Leyland Motors had never been in doubt. However, 1932's lone double-decker was not a Titan but a Short-bodied Daimler CP6 — perhaps a warning to Leyland not to take Tracky's orders for granted. Six coaches with Brush 'sunshine top' bodies delivered in 1933 and widely used that summer on Peak District tours also used the CP6 chassis. Another unfamiliar make appeared in 1933, when Dennis supplied three examples of the Lancet, its Leyland Lion equivalent.

Cubs with 20-seat Roe bodies — destined to be the last small buses for more than 50 years — and six Tiger TS6 coaches bodied by fellow TBAT subsidiary Eastern Counties of Lowestoft.

'Oil' (diesel) engines, which offered greatly improved fuel economy, were now growing in popularity, and in 1933 Tracky had one installed in a 1930 Titan. The trial was an overwhelming success, as future orders were to confirm.

Three years after the company had replaced its own trams, Tracky buses replaced the ill-fated Dearne District Light Railways. The DDLR was in effect an inter-urban tramway, running from a terminus by the Alhambra Theatre in Barnsley to Thurnscoe, with short spurs from Wath to Manvers and to the Woodman Inn at Swinton. A financial disaster for the four Urban District Councils which operated it, the tramway should never have been built; parallel motor-bus services were already in operation when it opened in July 1924, and with its single-track layout with passing loops it could never have competed effectively. In recognition of this an arrangement to pool mileage and fares was negotiated with Yorkshire Traction in 1929, but the writing was on the wall, and in 1933 the councils sold the DDLR to Tracky for £75,000. The trams (an unnecessarily large fleet of 30, all single-deck, and referred to as 'railcars') ceased running at the end of September. Some bus services were adjusted, but no direct replacement was needed. The 'car barns' in Brampton Road then served as Tracky's Wombwell depot for the next 67 years, being rebuilt and expanded during the 1950s. The DDLR was a tragic case of misplaced optimism and wasted investment, but its demise suited Yorkshire Traction.

The most important 1930s takeovers involved Lancashire & Yorkshire Motors of Shafton, Edward Mills of Hoyle Mill and Charles Wray of Lundwood and took effect from November 1934. In total 25 assorted vehicles were acquired, increasing the Tracky fleet to around 250. All three operators were members of the Pontefract Road Bus Owners' Association and ran from Barnsley to Grimethorpe, L&Y running additionally to Pontefract, whilst both L&Y and Mills also ran coastal expresses. Following the takeovers Tracky had a dominant position on Pontefract Road, (as it had in the rest of the Barnsley urban area) and a depot at Shafton, inherited from L&Y.

In 1935 activity centred on the Skellow area, north of Doncaster, where the aim was to co-ordinate services with those of Doncaster Corporation Transport. Tracky acquired B&E's Doncaster–Skellow service (with a Lion and a Tiger), followed by T. S. Camplejohn's Doncaster–Ackworth service (and another

Bodied by Brush, they were followed in 1934 by a further 20, all but one bodied by Charles Roe of Leeds; the exception had an early metal-framed Metro-Cammell body. The Daimlers were not a great success, and no more were ordered, but some of the Lancets survived to work alongside postwar equivalents bought in 1950.

Leyland still won some orders, including 14 Lions for bodying by Roe in 1933/4. Until 1933 Roe had not supplied bodywork to Tracky, but it quickly became a firm favourite. As a TBAT subsidiary Tracky had no loyalty to local manufacturers, and in any case the nearest Yorkshire had to a major chassis builder was Karrier of Huddersfield, and Karriers were never popular with the major groups; Tracky ran 10 at various times, all from acquired operators. Other Leylands delivered during this period were eight

Thirty-six new diesel-engined Leylands delivered in 1935 marked the start of Tracky's 'glory days'. First to arrive was 438 (HE 6654), a Titan TD3c with torque-converter automatic transmission and Brush side-gangway bodywork, the only double-decker to join the fleet between 1932 and 1937. This posed shot shows it ready to enter service, its attractive lines marred only by the front destination equipment, which looks like an afterthought. In 1940 it was fitted with a normal gearbox, and in 1946 the original body was replaced by a considerably less attractive effort by Strachans, as shown on page 21. *Author's collection*

five vehicles) and finally Marson's Owston Park service, enabling the co-ordination agreement to take effect from November. Another three vehicles came from Bates of Mexborough, but after 1935 only four more operators were acquired before the war, these being minor concerns involved mainly in colliery transport. Since 1929 more than 70 vehicles had been taken into stock from acquired businesses, and for a time the maintenance staff, previously used only to Leylands, had to contend with an incredible array of vehicles from ADC, AEC, AJS, Albion, Chevrolet, Daimler, Dennis, Gilford, GMC, Guy, Karrier, Maudslay, Renault, REO, Star and Thornycroft, all with their particular quirks. Most didn't last long.

After the Daimlers and Dennises Tracky resumed its loyalty to Leyland in 1935 and for the rest of the decade bought only Tigers and Titans. These were magnificent — superbly engineered, finished to a high standard of comfort and beautifully presented. The 'glory days' had arrived!

Tigers were now also bought for bus work, and by 1940 a huge fleet of 184 diesel-engined 32-seaters would be built up. Deliveries in 1935 were of TS7s, bodied by Leyland and Weymann (10 each) and Roe (15). Another 60 followed in 1936/7, with Roe bodies apart from four bodied by ECW (the new name for Eastern Counties' bodybuilding operation), while 59 TS8s with a mix of ECW and Roe bodywork came in 1938/9.

The balance of the 1935 deliveries were TS7 Tigers, numbered 470-504. No 471 (HE 6741) was one of 10 with 32-seat BET-style Weymann bodywork, the others being bodied by Leyland (10) and Roe (15). It is shown here, soon after delivery, at Midland Red's Southgate Street garage in Leicester, a stop on the Yorkshire Services 'Midland Route' from Yorkshire to London. Although the Tigers were intended primarily as service buses, their quality of finish and standard of comfort made them perfectly acceptable for occasional long-distance work. *G. F. H. Atkins*

Roe-bodied 503 (HE 6773) looks truly magnificent in its original livery as it stands outside the Yorkshire Traction office at Waterdale, Doncaster (telephone 1332). The commendably comprehensive blind display for the 75-minute journey to Barnsley on service 22 lists six intermediate points, including 'Conisboro' and 'Mexboro'; the 22 was a direct forerunner of today's 222 but ran via Manvers Main rather than Swinton. No 503 kept its original body until withdrawn in 1950, although seven of the batch would be rebodied that year, lasting until 1958. *G. F. H. Atkins*

They brought a high level of standardisation and sophistication, and although most were broadly similar in outline there were variations in appearance, and later batches wore a 'streamlined' livery evocative of the period.

Double-deck deliveries in the later '30s were also diesel-engined and comprised a lone 'gearless' TD3c with Brush bodywork in 1935 and 12 Roe-bodied TD5s to replace the earliest TD1s in 1938/9. The TD5s had central upstairs gangways, being Tracky's first buses of this layout.

Several acquired operators had held licences for seasonal services to Blackpool — *the* destination for those from the West Riding who could afford a holiday. Since 1933 the major Yorkshire operators, together with Ribble Motor Services and three Blackpool independents, had been discussing a rationalisation of services between Yorkshire and the Lancashire resort. The outcome was a new pattern of joint services from 1935, when Tracky acquired four coaches from the Blackpool operators — two Tigers from Walker Taylor & Sons, who traded as Pride of

the Road (a name we shall hear again), and an AEC Regal and an Albion Valiant from Armitage's Progress Motors.

At about this time Tracky was instrumental in BET's acquisition of several Sheffield-area coach operators, which were merged in 1935 under the Sheffield United Tours title. Yorkshire Traction, East Midland and North Western were the major shareholders, but SUT, as it became widely known, was managed as a separate concern.

New coaches in the late 1930s were Burlingham-bodied Tigers — eight TS7s in 1936/7, probably petrol-engined (and, if so, certainly Tracky's last such vehicles), and nine TS8s in 1938/9. The earlier Tiger coaches had rather short lives, the TS2s having all been sold by 1937.

The big event of 1938 was the opening in December of the 27-stand 'Barnsley Omnibus Station', on former railway land between the lines to Sheffield from Court House and Exchange stations. It was used by all Tracky services from the town, as well as by the Yorkshire Services, and replaced various town-centre termini (Eldon Street had been a major departure point, but the

Pontefract Road services, for example, had run from Gas Nook). Before long all the independent operators were also using the bus station, which soon came to be recognised as one of the finest in the North of England.

George Robinson died in April 1939, having been General Manager since the latter days of B&D and overseen a doubling of the company's size. His replacement, Norman Dean, joined Tracky in June and went on to become the longest-serving General Manager, retiring in 1965. He came from BET's Hebble Motor Services at Halifax, having been there since 1922, when it was an independent family business run by the Holdsworth brothers. No sooner had he got his feet under the table than war broke out, and from 16 September services were drastically curtailed.

The fleet at the end of 1939 stood at 286, with an impressive average age of just over four years. Most were single-deck buses, but there were also around 40 coaches — some converted to ambulances ready for the crisis ahead — and 20 double-deckers. The oldest were 1930 Lions, and only 10 were second-hand. The fleet was as well placed as it could possibly be to go to war.

3. War and peace

At the outbreak of war Tracky had a fleet to be proud of, and 30 Tiger TS8s and six Titan TD5s with prewar-specification ECW bodies which arrived early in 1940 were the icing on the cake. However, the enforced service cuts and suspension of coach activities meant that fewer vehicles were needed. Many were delicensed, and in the spring and early summer of 1940 — after losing many vehicles at Dunkirk — the military authorities impressed more than 40 single-deckers, fortunately leaving the front-line fleet of Tigers intact. In some cases Tracky also provided drivers. Other vehicles were lent to operators that were struggling to cope, and for a time nearly all the Dennis Lancets were in use elsewhere; West Riding had five at Castleford, and Chester-based Crosville Motor Services and the Northern Ireland Road Transport Board had eight apiece. Crosville also had at least three TD1s, and Tracky assisted Sheffield Corporation after the disastrous bombing raids of December 1940. Most of the loaned vehicles returned in 1941/2, but some that went to the military were never seen again.

In August 1940 two operators sharing the Barnsley–Dodworth service with Tracky sold out, each with a second-hand Leyland Lion, Thomas Darlow's having come from Yorkshire Woollen, while Mrs Lockwood's late husband had bought theirs from West Riding. Two months later Sydney McAdoo of Cudworth sold Tracky his 'Pioneer' services from Barnsley to Fitzwilliam and Thurnscoe, together with a Karrier Chaser and three Albions. These were the only wartime takeovers.

The Regional Transport Commissioners now determined which services should operate and how often, and in 1940, as the fuel shortage temporarily eased, they allowed some Tracky services to be reinstated. That summer coastal expresses took holidaymakers to Blackpool, Cleethorpes, Scarborough and Skegness, but they would not be so lucky in 1941.

Operators could not order vehicles in the usual way and got what the Ministry of War Transport allocated, even if normally this would have been woefully inadequate. Tracky got nothing in 1941 and in 1942 received just one Titan — an 'unfrozen' TD7 built from stock parts, with a grey-painted highbridge Roe body. There was no shortage of buses overall, but only the 26 double-deckers

had more than 32 seats, so high-capacity vehicles were desperately needed; with so many staff having enlisted, manning duplicates was almost impossible. An unpopular short-term measure involved single-deckers' operating with all seats facing inwards, backs to the windows, to create a large central standing area.

More new double-deckers were allocated in 1943, but instead of the sophisticated Titans that Norman Dean would have liked (after completing the 'unfrozen' buses Leyland built no more for the rest of the war) these were totally unfamiliar Guy Arabs, with six-cylinder Gardner engines and 'utility' bodywork. Two came in early 1943, one with a lowbridge Weymann body and the other a highbridge body by Massey of Wigan. Eighteen Mk IIs would follow by 1945, four with lowbridge Roe bodywork, the rest with highbridge bodies from Massey, Northern Counties, Park Royal and Weymann. The Chairman, J. S. Wills, based at BET head-quarters in London and therefore a step removed from day-to-day management, publicly expressed his regret that the Guys, with their hard seats, failed to match Tracky's normal standards of comfort.

Wills was also unhappy that some buses had to be converted to run on 'producer' gas. The gas buses towed an anthracite-burning trailer, reducing dependence on imported fuel, but their dismal performance meant they could operate only the flattest routes.

▲ Leyland Titan TD7 703 (HE 9713) was assembled from 'unfrozen' Leyland parts, but its Roe bodywork was clearly to 'utility' specification, having none of the elegance of the Roe-bodied TD5s of the late 1930s. The grey livery in which it was delivered in 1942 didn't help, but it looked considerably better in standard livery, as seen here on 6 August 1956. The photograph shows it about to leave Barnsley bus station for Park House Estate (which later came to be regarded as part of Kendray), with one of the former SUT AEC Regal coaches in the background. *John Cockshott Archive*

Twenty 'utility' Guy Arabs, including 15 highbridge buses, arrived between early 1943 and the end of the war. Showing off its austere lines at Huddersfield in March 1952, 719 (HE 9916), dating from 1944, was one of four to keep their original Northern Counties highbridge bodies until the end, which in this case came with withdrawal in 1957. The lack of destination or number blinds was unfortunate on a rear-entrance bus. Sharing the parking ground are a prewar Leyland Tiger and, on the left, an intruder from Lancashire —a 1949 Bolton Corporation Crossley with 'Special' on its blind. *John Fozard*

More than 25 petrol-engined buses were converted, but there were no regrets when the Government ended the scheme in 1944. A better way to reduce fuel consumption was to extend the use of diesel, and between 1944 and 1946 a dozen Lancets were fitted with Gardner 5LWs in lieu of their Dennis petrol units, while the TS6 Tigers received Leyland diesels.

Another 'invisible' ownership change occurred in 1942 when TBAT, the alliance between Tilling and BET, was dissolved. Tracky reverted to the BET group, but the railway shareholdings continued unchanged.

As if life were not difficult enough, a major strike over pay and conditions began in May 1943. Norman Dean told the *Sheffield Star* on 12 May that he had been informed just after midnight, following a mass meeting held at 11pm. The strike was not supported by the Transport & General Workers' Union but was absolutely solid, and no buses ran that day. Cleaners and fitters also came out. Other local operators were also affected, including Huddersfield, Rotherham and Sheffield corporations, County Motors, Mexborough & Swinton and even smaller concerns, such as T. Burrows & Sons at Wombwell. With many essential pit and munitions workers unable to get to work the Government was forced into decisive action. Within two days the Ministry of

War Transport drafted in a large fleet of lorries to transport workers and schoolchildren, the personnel involved setting up camp in Barnsley. Later about 15 coaches (commandeered, no doubt, like the lorries) arrived, probably for use on normal public services. The strike was long and bitter — the longest in Tracky's history — and was not settled until 2 June, well after most other operators' staff had returned to work. The army vehicles covered more than 140,000 miles replacing Yorkshire Traction services, a major distraction from the main thrust of the war effort.

Only one Tracky bus suffered bomb damage, at least on home territory, this being sustained in Doncaster in December 1940; some passengers were hurt, but the bus was repairable. More serious was the damage to 1940 Tiger 688, which careered off the road near Harley in 1944, damaging the body beyond economic repair. The outcome was a 'new' Leyland double-decker, achieved by marrying the Short body from the 1932 Daimler CP6 with the Leyland chassis.

For much of the war passengers were bombarded with requests to avoid unnecessary journeys (or not to travel at all), and six years of pent-up demand was suddenly released when it ended. Like other operators, Tracky came under huge pressure, but an immediate reversion to prewar service levels was out of the

question. Even so, thanks to a superhuman effort by the staff,
mileage operated in 1947 exceeded the busiest prewar year (1938),
and passenger numbers had rocketed by almost 50%. Several
years passed before all services were 'normal' again; the through
Sheffield–Barnsley–Leeds/Bradford services, for example, were
not reinstated until 1949.

The fleet had taken a battering. Instead of around 30 new buses
a year only 21 were received in total between 1941 and 1945, and
many older vehicles, including venerable centre-entrance Lions,
had been given an extra lease of life through the ingenuity of staff
at the Central Works at Upper Sheffield Road. At the end of the
war around 310 vehicles were owned, but many were non-
runners, having been kept in case the situation deteriorated
further and in order to avoid the red tape associated with selling
them. (Aside from those going for military use only about 10
were sold between 1940 and 1944, including the ex-McAdoo
Albion Victor, which went to Mexborough & Swinton in 1941,
and a Cub sold to Baddeley's at Holmfirth in 1944, in which year
the last six TD1s were also sold.)

New buses were desperately needed, and quickly, but only
Leylands would do. The first to arrive, in the summer of 1946,
were five Titan PD1s with highbridge Roe bodies, possibly
delivered against an earlier order as the 'unfrozen' TD7 was the
only evidence so far of six Leyland double-deckers reputedly
expected during the war. Nos 725-9 were distinguished by their
three-letter registrations (AHE 162-6), Barnsley's original 'HE'

series having been completed soon after delivery of the last Guy,
724 (HE 9978), early in 1945; 10,000 motor vehicles had now been
registered in the borough! The only other new double-deckers
during the 1940s were highbridge buses on Titan PD2/1 chassis:
five with Leyland bodies in 1948 and six with Roe in 1949.

Single-deckers were still the mainstay of the fleet (without all
those low bridges Tracky's profit margins would have been
healthier still!), and 45 Tiger PS1s with 32-seat BET-style
forward-entrance bodies by Roe (22) and Weymann (23) arrived
in 1947. Another 48 Tigers came in 1949, Brush-bodied PS1s but
for two exceptions; 780 had Tracky's only single-deck body from
Northern Coachbuilders (a small Tyneside-based outfit not to be
confused with Northern Counties of Wigan, which bodied many
Tracky buses), while 810 had the 9.8-litre O.600 engine rather
than the usual 7.4-litre E181 unit, making it Tracky's only
bus-bodied PS2. This bus was exhibited at the 1949 Commercial
Motor Show and featured fluorescent interior lighting, then quite
revolutionary. The new Tigers allowed the last Lions to be
withdrawn in 1949, and the only vehicle from an acquired
operator to survive into the 1950s was a former Pride of the Road
Tiger, now with later bodywork.

From January 1948 there was a significant 'behind the scenes'
ownership change when Clement Attlee's Labour Government
nationalised the railways and their bus-company shareholdings,
giving the state-owned British Transport Commission a 49%
stake in Tracky.

The first new postwar deliveries marked a reversion to Leylands —
five 'crash-gearbox' Titan PD1s with attractive Roe 56-seat bodies
(725-9), delivered in 1946. No 728 (AHE 165) shows the 'H' fleet-
number suffix, added slightly later to distinguish buses which could
be used only on routes that were free of low bridges. It is waiting
at the Central Station terminus in Doncaster, before operating to
Sprotbrough on service 49. The route out of Doncaster would take
it over North Bridge, then still part of the A1 Great North Road and
carrying heavy long-distance traffic — as well as Doncaster CT
trolleybuses on the Bentley service. *M. A. Taylor*

The first single-deckers
'upgraded' with new bodies
after the end of the war were
four 1935 Tiger TS7s fitted with
new 'semi-utility' Strachans
bodies in 1946. The new bodies
replaced the Leyland originals,
which were far more stylish
but structurally unsound.
One of them is seen bearing left
into Regent Street *en route*
for Barnsley bus station, as a
wartime Guy heads the other
way. All four buses were
scrapped in 1953. *Barnsley
Archives and Local Studies*

Also placed in service in 1946 was 438 (HE 6654) with its new lowbridge Strachans body. This was essentially to utility specification and in stark contrast to the elegant original of 1935 (see page 14) but was good enough to allow 438 to put in another 11 years' service. Here it stands in Barnsley bus station before a trip via Barugh Green to Kexborough (here spelled 'Kexborough', as in Mexborough — a constant source of confusion locally) on service 92. The bus to the right — whatever it may be — is very obviously of superior construction. The figures in the background give this view a slightly eerie quality, yet the shadow on the ground shows that the sun is breaking through. *Author's collection; source unknown*

In 1949 six 1935/6 Titan TD4s with wartime lowbridge bodies came as a stopgap from Hebble, Norman Dean's former company; the first second-hand buses since 1921 other than those from acquired businesses, they retained their original Hebble numbers between 121 and 134 instead of being numbered in Tracky's usual series, which by now had reached 779.

As a further measure to modernise the fleet several Tiger TS7s were rebodied, producing what looked like brand-new buses for less than half the cost. Four Leyland-bodied buses of 1935 were dealt with by Strachans in 1946, and in 1947/8 Charles Roberts of Wakefield rebodied the coaches, which in rebuilt form were diesel-powered. Two double-deckers were also rebodied, both to lowbridge layout. The lone 1935 Titan (which back in 1940 had lost its torque-converter in favour of conventional gears) had its Brush original replaced by Strachans in 1946, while 722, the double-deck Tiger, received a new Roe body in 1949.

Other vehicles received older bodies, the remaining six TS7s with Leyland's troublesome metal-framed bodywork gaining the 1933 Brush bodies from the Daimler CP6s in 1946, rebuilt for bus use after wartime service as ambulances. A 1940 Tiger (676) was notable in having its original ECW body replaced by a 1934 Roe body after an accident in 1946 and later receiving a third body, this time becoming a coach!

Once again Leyland Motors was enjoying a clean sweep of Tracky's chassis orders, but worldwide demand for Leyland vehicles was enormous, and Tracky was forced to look elsewhere to maintain fleet renewal. The last vehicles bought in preference to Leylands had been the Dennis Lancets of 1933/4, sturdy machines which matched or even bettered the Tigers for longevity. Dennis was the obvious choice, and 30 Lancet IIIs were ordered. The first six, with stylish Windover Huntingdon bodies, gave the coach fleet a much-needed boost when they entered service in the summer of 1949; until now coach operations, which had resumed in 1946, had been undertaken either by prewar vehicles (including the 1934 Tiger TS6s, most of which had been specially refurbished) or by buses. Things were starting to look up.

Single-deckers far outnumbered double-deckers in the late 1940s, and 104 Tiger PS1s with 32-seat BET-style bodies arrived between 1947 and 1950. Four manufacturers were involved in supplying the bodywork, and 730-52 (AHE 461-83) of 1947 had Weymann bodies. Although modified to become 34-seaters in 1950, they were all withdrawn within nine years for rebodying as double-deckers; 734 re-emerged in early 1955 as Roe-bodied 1040 (HHE 321), its single-deck body being sold. It is seen in August 1952 in St Sepulchre Gate, about to reach Doncaster (Central) station, terminus of the hourly 14A service to Goldthorpe via Marr and Hickleton. *John Fozard*

Another 22 Tigers (753-74) delivered in 1947 had Roe bodywork, and all but two led full lives as single-deckers. No 770 (AHE 792) is seen in Lord Street, Huddersfield, with passengers already on board for a journey on service 86A to Holmfirth, then a workaday Pennine town unmarred by television-inspired tourism. Behind, and looking considerably older, is Sheffield Joint Omnibus Committee 146 (KWJ 146), a 1948 Weymann-bodied AEC Regal, which will also run via Waterloo and Shepley as it heads south towards its home city on service 68. This was jointly worked with Tracky and low bridges in the Penistone area dictated single-deck operation. *Roy Marshall*

No 780 (BHE 441) was unique among Tracky's PS1s in having a body by Northern Coachbuilders, although, given that this was to BET design standards, it hardly stood out from the crowd. Here it poses in the sun outside Oakes Café ('Transport drivers' Bed & Breakfast') at Waterdale, Doncaster, after the short run in from Sprotbrough on service 49. After withdrawal from normal service in 1960 No 780 was modified to carry disabled passengers on behalf of the County Borough of Barnsley, receiving a mainly cream livery with the Barnsley municipal crest. In this form it lasted until 1966, still owned by Tracky. *Author's collection; source unknown*

More TS7s were rebodied over the winter of 1947/8, the 1937/8 coaches losing their original Burlingham bodies in favour of new bus bodies by Roberts of Wakefield. Roberts was better known as a builder of tramcars and railway wagons and produced few single-deck buses after the war; these eight were possibly the only examples to BET design and lasted until 1957. No 580 (HE 7776), a 1937 vehicle believed to have been fitted originally with a petrol engine, is seen at Huddersfield in March 1952, on layover before a journey to Denby Dale via Kirkburton. *John Fozard*

23

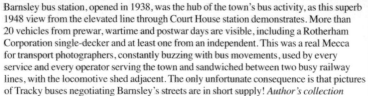

Barnsley bus station, opened in 1938, was the hub of the town's bus activity, as this superb 1948 view from the elevated line through Court House station demonstrates. More than 20 vehicles from prewar, wartime and postwar days are visible, including a Rotherham Corporation single-decker and at least one from an independent. This was a real Mecca for transport photographers, constantly buzzing with bus movements, used by every service and every operator serving the town and sandwiched between two busy railway lines, with the locomotive shed adjacent. The only unfortunate consequence is that pictures of Tracky buses negotiating Barnsley's streets are in short supply! *Author's collection*

The first of what was to become a fleet of 75 PD2s arrived in the spring of 1948. Nos 775-9 were PD2/1s with 56-seat Leyland highbridge bodies, and 779 (BHE 140) is seen in Lord Street, Huddersfield, before returning to Barnsley on service 15. The large rectangular 'Clayton' blind equipment accommodated a single linen blind, combining the service number with the destination and intermediate points in such a way that it could be used for journeys in either direction, here showing '15 Barnsley and Huddersfield via Staincross'. In the background an inspector observes the photographer's actions. *John Fozard*

Roe-bodied Titans 828-33 arrived in late 1949, and 832 (BHE 762) is seen here in Barnsley bus station, operating service 4 to Worsbrough Common (appearing on the single-line destination blind as Worsboro' Common). A thick coating of grime — probably containing a substantial element of coal dust — has obliterated the fleetname, but Charles Roe's factory transfer remains visible below the driver's cab window. The advertisement was created for days like this ('When life is grim try Holland's gin … have a De Kuyper'); the fug upstairs can just be imagined, with pipes and Woodbines lit after a shift down the pit. Most passengers are wearing either headsquares or cloth caps. *Photobus*

No doubt Norman Dean would have been acutely embarrassed by this distinctly shabby specimen, especially as it represented his former company! To address the urgent need for double-deckers the unprecedented step was taken of acquiring six Titan TD4s from Hebble in early 1949. Nos 121-4/6/34 dated from 1935/6 but had wartime bodies and lasted for up to four years with Tracky. In this view at North Bridge, Doncaster, Willowbrook-bodied 122 (JX 2535) awaits passengers on the two-hourly 94A, which combined with the 94 via Barnsdale Bar to give an hourly frequency through to Upton. *Author's collection; source unknown*

To help get coach operations going again after the war most of the 1934 Tiger TS6/Eastern Counties coaches, now fitted with diesel engines, were refurbished, resulting in an attractive but quite different appearance. No 430 (HE 6343) is seen here at Waterdale, Doncaster, *en route* for Birmingham. These vehicles were 20 years old when finally displaced by modern underfloor-engined coaches in 1954. Distances within England's largest county can be vast; Sheffield is closer to Birmingham than it is to Scarborough, while Barnsley is almost as close to Blackpool as it is to the East Coast resort. *J. Joyce / Online Transport Archive*

Six 1949 Dennis Lancets with elegant Windover Huntingdon bodies (872-7) were the first new postwar coaches. Although founded in 1796, Windover apparently sprang from nowhere in the decade after the war to produce distinctive coach bodies, including to BET and Tilling customers. For a time it was Tracky's favourite supplier, providing the company with more coaches between 1949 and 1953 than Duple, probably Britain's best-known coachbuilder, managed in its entire history! No 877 (CHE 380) is seen in August 1953 at Victoria Coach Station, London, about to be refuelled after a 'Midland Route' journey from Yorkshire. Its registration was replicated in 1972 on a Leyland Leopard service bus, but with a 'K' suffix. *John Fozard*

4. The 1950s

Postwar passenger growth continued into the 1950s, and in the early part of the decade all efforts were focussed on keeping pace with demand. Passenger journeys had risen from 42.3 million in 1938 to a staggering 76.6 million — almost a million and a half a week — in 1950

At the start of 1950 more than 80% of the fleet was single-deck, and there were only 16 postwar double-deckers. Despite the bridge problem Norman Dean was not happy with side-gangway double-deckers — they were unpopular with passengers and conductors — and preferred single-deckers for restricted routes. Now, however, in the quest for additional capacity and greater efficiency, double-deckers gained wider acceptance, and by mid-1951 46 Titan PD2/1s had arrived, followed by the end of 1953 by 29 of the longer and wider PD2/12 model. Body orders were shared between Leyland, Northern Counties and Roe, and more than half were of lowbridge layout. There were now more than 120 double-deckers, compared with just 36 a decade earlier.

The large prewar fleet of Leyland diesels survived intact into the 1950s, albeit with a few of the Tigers sporting new bodies, but many had visibly seen better days. Double-deckers included the ECW-bodied Titan TD5s of 1940 (661-6), and 665 (HE 9519) was found at New Lodge in September 1951, after the photographer had cycled from Leeds. Its blinds suggest a journey from Barnsley to Cundy Cross via Stairfoot, while the painted advertisements either side of the destination screen illustrate the evolution of the English language by urging the citizens of Barnsley to 'Go Gay at Butlins'. The terraced housing in the background is in Wakefield Road. *Colin Routh*

The PD2s were solid and dependable and formed the backbone of the double-deck fleet until well into the 1960s, becoming familiar across almost the whole network and especially on the trunk services radiating out across the West Riding to Bradford, Leeds, Pontefract, Doncaster, Sheffield and Huddersfield.

On the single-deck front a revolution in design was just around the corner, and Tracky's last half-cabs — 24 Dennis Lancets and 12 Tiger PS1s with BET-style Brush saloon bodies, and six Windover-bodied Tiger PS2/3 coaches — came in 1950.

Rebodying continued, a final dozen prewar Tiger TS7s receiving new Weymann saloon bodies in 1950 (among them 492, of which

more later). Attention then turned to the utility Guys, whose rugged chassis and Gardner engines would clearly outlast the bodywork. Lowbridge Roe bodies were fitted to 704-9 in 1950, while 710-5 gained highbridge equivalents in 1952; the others survived in broadly original form until withdrawn.

The huge intake of new vehicles (167 in the years 1949-51 alone) brought fleet strength up to about 380 but also replaced many older vehicles. The final prewar Lancets went in 1951, and by the end of 1954 the only surviving prewar Tiger buses were those rebodied by Roberts and Weymann; even Strachans' efforts of 1946 lasted only seven years.

The first new buses of the decade were 844-7, all-Leyland Titan PD2/1s which entered service in January 1950. They were the first side-gangway buses since the war; this layout was not ideal, but in an area dogged by low railway bridges its adoption allowed many services to be converted to double-deck operation. These included the Pontefract Road routes out of Barnsley, on which 845 (CHE 194) is seen in Hemsworth, heading for Upton. The superb array of advertisements alongside the bus dates the picture to 1957, and the Barnsley vs Bristol City match at Oakwell on 30 November resulted in a 4-1 win for Barnsley, who were thrashed 7-0 away at Cardiff a week later! The adverts on the front of 845 have a seasonal flavour — 'VP wine at Turkey time'. *A. B. Cross*

Other Titans of 1950 included Tracky's only examples with Roe lowbridge bodies (878-84). No 879 (CHE 610) is seen soon after delivery in Castlegate, Sheffield, about to leave for Upton on service 70, with a circle containing the letters 'LB' to the right of the blind aperture to denote its lowbridge status, rather than an 'L' suffix to the fleet number, as used later. This was a joint operation with the Sheffield JOC, and the journey took two minutes short of two hours, with a 10-minute rest at Wombwell. Passing in the opposite direction on service 87 to Maltby is Sheffield Corporation's 525 (HWB 825), a 1946 Daimler CWA6. *V. C. Jones*

Another 10 Titan PD2/1s, with classic highbridge Leyland bodywork, arrived in the spring of 1950 as 834-43, and 836 (BHE 766) is seen here awaiting passengers for Kirkburton in Lord Street, Huddersfield, with the Palace cinema as a backdrop. The original Clayton blind aperture is not used here to full advantage and would later be replaced with separate apertures for destination and number blinds. Barnsley & District had started running to Kirkburton in 1925, and five years later the LMS branch line from Huddersfield to the village closed. Again there are advertisements for 'VP wonderful wine', then the height of sophistication — Sauvignon Blanc was unheard of in those days!
S. J. Butler collection

A fine study of the rear of an all-Leyland PD2 as 837 (BHE 767) passes under the wires of the newly electrified Worsbrough branch, used mainly by heavy coal trains travelling from Wath Yard across to Lancashire, at Worsbrough Bridge. The bus is about to start the long slog up the A61 to the Cutting End and could well be operating the lengthy Sheffield–Barnsley–Bradford (66) or Leeds (67) services. Variety in the Yorkshire brewing industry is evident: the Ship Inn advertises Melbourne Ales from Leeds, while 837 promotes Hammonds of Huddersfield, at a time when Barnsley-brewed Oakwell ales or Clarksons' beers were the main choice in the town.
John Fozard

The final PD2/1s, 929-42, were all-Leyland lowbridge buses delivered in 1951. No 929 (DHE 567) was for many years based at Doncaster, and this May 1959 view shows it freshly repainted, beside the market hall in Oxford Road, Mexborough; from here it would turn right into Station Road. Its destination is Barnsley, but careless setting of the blinds leaves some doubt as to whether this is a 22 or a 22A — if you were heading for Brampton it made all the difference! *Roger Holmes*

In 1953 came 10 Leyland PD2/12s (977-86) with Northern Counties lowbridge bodywork featuring a pronounced curve to the front profile. This was the first time Tracky had *chosen* this builder's products, earlier examples being on wartime Guys. No 982 (EHE 929) is seen at stand 23 in Barnsley bus station before leaving for Doncaster on 'main road' service 14, which followed the A635 all the way, taking 48 minutes. In the background is Larratt Pepper's 1955 AEC Reliance/Willowbrook PWR 403 on the stage-carriage service to Thurnscoe, in this case one of the infrequent journeys serving the pit at Little Houghton. Larratt Pepper's service, which always employed single-deckers, would eventually be taken over by Tracky in 1978. *Photobus*

The combination of Dennis Lancet III chassis and BET-style bodywork was unique to Tracky. Twenty-four Brush-bodied Lancets (848-71) delivered in 1950 were the first Dennis buses for 16 years — and would be the last for another 40. Although non-standard, they led full and active lives, and with their large Dennis diesel engines outperformed the far more numerous Leyland PS1s. No 858 (CHE 350) is seen at Lower Mosley Street coach station in Manchester — always a hive of activity — after operating service 20 from Barnsley via the Woodhead Pass on 24 May 1958, with a rebodied prewar North Western Bristol K, due to leave for Hayfield via New Mills, in the background. *John Kaye*

School bus duties are often overlooked but were an integral part of Tracky's daily activities. This scene, dating probably from the late 1950s, shows Dennis Lancet 851 (CHE 343) collecting pupils from the village school at Birdsedge for the afternoon run to Denby Dale — and not a parental car in sight! Birdsedge is about four miles from Penistone in the direction of Huddersfield, and the school, which is still open, is situated just off one of the most exposed stretches of the A629 Sheffield–Huddersfield road. *John Fozard*

Contemporaries of the Lancets were the final Tiger PS1s (885-96), which had similar Brush bodies, but the painted Leyland radiator grilles and lower bonnet lines somehow gave them a less-intimidating appearance. Within a couple of years of delivery in 1950 both types were thoroughly obsolete, yet they survived until 1961/2. No 887 (CHE 721) labours up the gradient from Fir Vale to Pitsmoor in August 1959, with Firth Park Road in the distance, towards the end of a two-hour run from Upton to Sheffield on service 70, as a prewar Wolseley overtakes on the tram tracks. Like many of the Tigers, 887 was to become a works bus after sale, in this case for Tarmac. *R. F. Mack*

▲ Peak summer demand on the coastal express services far outstripped the capacity of the coach fleet, and in the early 1950s the Tiger PS1 buses frequently helped out. Here we see four Brush-bodied examples at the Coliseum coach station in Blackpool, 825 (BHE 755) and the two on the left having operated the J7 from Doncaster (but probably only as duplicates from Barnsley), while 891 (CHE 725) has its blinds set for the J11 to High Green, which ran via Penistone, Barnsley and Chapeltown. *M. A. Taylor*

▲ Tracky's only postwar Tiger coaches were six 1950 PS2/3s (897-902) with Windover Huntingdon bodies similar to those on the Lancets but with additional trim below the windows. On a quiet day in April 1957 No 898 (CHE 853) passes under the tram wires outside Sheffield Midland station as it heads south on the 'Ten Cities Express' to Coventry. Whilst the station façade remains largely unchanged today, except for cleaning to tackle its blackened appearance, the skyline was drastically altered in the early 1960s, when the now-listed Park Hill flats replaced slum housing, and the Cosy Café on the left has long since disappeared. No 897 would be withdrawn in 1960, its chassis forming the basis of a new double-decker, 1188 (THE 188). *R. F. Mack*

In all 24 TS7s were fitted postwar with new 34-seat bodies, twelve 1935/6 vehicles rebodied by Weymann completing the programme in 1950. Among these was 504 (HE 6774), which originally carried a Roe body (see picture of 503 on page 15). To the casual eye it looks like a brand-new bus as it awaits passengers at stand 2 in Barnsley bus station for the local run to Kingstone, but the original registration and prewar style of radiator give the game away. Behind, heading for Pogmoor, is 578 (HE 7774), a 1937 bus with a 1948 Roberts body. Service numbers are not displayed on either bus, or on the information boards above the stand. *Author's collection; source unknown*

No 574 (HE 7770) was the last of the 1937 batch of TS7 Tiger buses, and had Roe bodywork. It is seen here at the top of Regent Street in Barnsley, facing the Town Hall, its destination blind apparently not reset for its outward journey from town. None of the 1937 buses was rebodied, and early in 1951 No 574 would be sold to Southdown, the attraction being its diesel engine; it was not used in service. *Barnsley Archives and Local Studies*

A quick glance at this photograph taken in Barnsley bus station on 6 July 1952 (notice the staff in summer uniforms outside the office and canteen building) might suggest one of Tracky's Roe-bodied TD5s, but look again! The extra axle reveals the subject to be 127 (DT 9642), the 1938 Leyland Titanic acquired four months earlier with Cawthorne's Woolley Colliery service, which it is still operating here. It was new to Doncaster Corporation, which had quite a *penchant* for Titanics, and was bought by Cawthorne in 1949. Although repainted in Tracky livery, 127 — numbered in the same series as the former Hebble Titans — would be withdrawn by the year end.
Roger Holmes

Cawthorne's other double-decker was every bit as remarkable. No 128 (KMA 570) was a 1948 Foden bought from the manufacturer in 1950 after use as a demonstration vehicle, but its lowbridge Willowbrook body had originated in 1945 on an earlier Foden chassis, which in turn emerged with Warrington Corporation carrying a mid-1930s body! No 128's most extraordinary feature was its Foden supercharged six-cylinder two-stroke diesel engine, which produced incredible sound-effects. The bus could hardly have been more out of place with Tracky yet survived until 1959, and from 1953 it was the only second-hand vehicle in the fleet. It is seen here at Waterdale, Doncaster, on 15 June 1958. *Roger Holmes*

Many independents continued to prosper within Tracky's area, but most ran only one or two services, and the potential to expand through takeover was limited. The first acquisition in more than a decade came in 1951 with the Barnsley–Grimethorpe operations of Marrison of Cudworth (Marrison's erstwhile colleagues in the 'United' association having sold out in the 1930s). Tracky inherited two early Leyland Tigers with Brighouse Motors bodies but sold them immediately. Disappointingly Marrison's, which ceased trading, sold its modern Plaxton-bodied Daimler and Foden coaches separately; they would have made a superb sight in Tracky livery.

The only other 1950s takeover involved the Barnsley–Woolley Colliery service of W. & A. Cawthorne of Barugh, in 1952, bringing Tracky two remarkable double-deckers. No 127 was a 1938 Leyland Titanic TT5 six-wheeler with Roe bodywork, which had come from Doncaster Corporation Transport in 1949, while 128 was a 1948 Foden with Fodens's own revolutionary two-stroke diesel engine and a Willowbrook side-gangway body

transferred from a 1945 prototype. Unfortunately the Titanic did not see the year out, despite being repainted in Tracky livery (and looking quite at home if you ignored the extra axle!), but the Foden ran until 1959, the most eccentric member of the fleet by a long margin. At the same time Cawthorne's coach operations passed to the Barnsley British Co-operative Society, which would also have taken on the bus service but for problems with transferring the licence.

Leyland was now offering the Royal Tiger, which, with the engine under the floor between the axles and potential for up to 44 seats, looked like the answer to some of Tracky's problems. Twenty Brush-bodied examples took to the road early in 1951, followed by six with Roe bodies in 1952 and 10 from Willowbrook in 1953. They were 43-seaters, giving a huge advantage over the Lancets and Tigers, which at best seated 34 and were immediately rendered obsolete.

There were also Royal Tiger coaches, with Windover Kingsway bodies — six centre-entrance versions in 1951 and three with

The 1952 Royal Tigers (959-64) had Roe bodywork and were to the new 8ft width limit. No 963 (EHE 164) stands on the forecourt of Barnsley depot, facing Upper Sheffield Road, with the head-office buildings on the right — notice the fine lamp bracket above the entrance to Pindar Oaks Garage! It was about to set off for the bus station to pick up a short working on service 30A, which followed a convoluted route via Pogmoor, Kingstone, Stairfoot and Cundy Cross to Athersley. In 1966 No 963 would be sold to Arthur Rowe of Cudworth, for use on his service from Barnsley to Royston via Cudworth and Shafton, which Tracky was to take over in 1969. *EPTG / Roy Marshall collection*

No 992 (EHE 939) was the first of the final series of Royal Tiger buses, a batch of 10 delivered in 1953 with the first bodies ordered by Tracky from Willowbrook of Loughborough. The location for this shot may be unknown, but there is no doubting the nature of the service ('Workmen' was a catch-all used by Tracky for any kind of works service, although invariably known to staff as 'paddy buses'; other operators made a point of showing 'Colliery Service', or words to that effect, for miners' services). No 992 was to end its days operating on hire to Mexborough & Swinton in 1968/9, by which time it had been renumbered 400.
S. J. Butler collection

rear entrances (designed to give passengers the best forward vision) in 1953. With the underfloor-engine layout coachbuilders exercised more influence over the overall appearance of vehicles, and some were apt to let their imaginations run wild. Windover, however, exercised some restraint and produced very modern-looking bodies without being too outrageous.

Many BET operators loved AECs, but they never gained a foothold in the Tracky fleet, so it came as quite a surprise when six 1947 Regals were acquired from Sheffield United Tours, entering service early in 1952. They were attractive coaches — and Tracky's first with Duple bodies — but lasted only until 1956.

Three 'new' coaches also arrived in 1952, supplied by Beadle of Rochester and based around recycled mechanical components from prewar Leyland Tiger TS8 coaches. Curiously, a final 'prewar' coach was created the same year by switching the 1938 Burlingham body from former Pride of the Road Tiger 466 onto the chassis of 1940 TS8 676, which had already carried two different bus bodies!

The coach fleet underwent a dramatic transformation after 1951, triggered by the arrival of six underfloor-engined Royal Tigers (923-8) with Windover Kingsway bodies; these represented a vast leap into the modern era compared with the previous year's Tiger PS2s, and the half-cab coach immediately looked dated. Nos 923-8 had 37-seat centre-entrance bodies, but another three Kingsways delivered in 1953 were 39-seaters, with the entrance positioned behind the rear wheels. This wintry scene shows 927 (DHE 565) parked at Huntingdon Street bus station in Nottingham, alongside a Trent single-decker. *W. J. Haynes*

No 924 of the same batch is seen at Waterdale, Doncaster, on 10 September 1959, on an excursion to the races. Apart from its railway works, Doncaster's main claim to fame was — and still is — as a racing town; its greatest race, the St Leger, is run in September, and 1959's winner was Cantelo. Particular care was taken with the appearance of coaches, with a winged monogram style of fleetname (quite unlike the prosaic style used on buses) and very discreet fleet numbers, just discernible here on the offside wing. In the background is a Bristol LS from the United fleet, giving its passengers a break on a long-distance express service between Tyneside and London. *Roger Holmes*

Tracky's appetite for Leylands meant that no new vehicles were ever bought from arch-rival AEC, although six 1947 Regals (HWJ 983-8) were acquired from Sheffield United Tours and placed in service for the 1952 season, numbered 965-70. Part of a batch of 25 with SUT, they put in five years' service with Tracky before being sold early in 1957 and snapped up by other operators which probably appreciated them more.
With 'Birmingham' displayed as its destination, 969 shows the elegant lines of the Duple A-type body. The only previous Regal in the fleet had come from Progress Motors of Blackpool in 1935 and ran until 1945. *S. J. Butler collection*

Three coaches (971-3) supplied in 1952 by Beadle of Dartford were also of the modern full-front style. In effect they were rebodied Tiger TS8s, although registered as new Beadle products. No 972 (EHE 382) owed its existence to 1939 Tiger 629 (HE 8919), which until 1951 had sported a Burlingham coach body. In this view outside Chambers Café at Waterdale, on 11 August 1953, its gleaming paintwork reflects the grille of nearly new Royal Tiger/Windover 974 (EHE 921) as both coaches await departure for Birmingham. Notice the very different livery applications. *Roger Holmes*

Six years on 972 was still performing regular express-service duties, being seen here passing through Harrogate in August 1959 on the 'Ten Cities Express' from Coventry to Newcastle via Birmingham, Lichfield, Derby, Sheffield, Wakefield, Leeds, Ripon and Durham (Derby was not yet a city, but 'Nine Cities Express' wouldn't have had the same ring to it!). Other traffic includes an early Morris Minor and a recent Ford Zodiac, while just visible in the distance is a Bristol/ECW double-decker of the West Yorkshire Road Car Co. *John Fozard*

Despite their advantages, the Royal Tigers were exceptionally heavy, and Norman Dean reported that fuel consumption on local services was no better than for double-deckers, and tyre wear worse. Leyland was already on the case and came up with the Tiger Cub, using smaller engines and lightweight construction. Orders were soon placed, 1002-28 arriving in 1954 with 'matching' registrations— something that would not be repeated for several years. Nos 1002-25 (GHE 2-25) had Saunders-Roe bus bodies, while 1026-8 (GHE 26-8) were Willowbrook-bodied coaches with rear entrances. Although employing bus-style body frames and lacking the flamboyance of the Windovers, they still had style.

Tracky took to the Tiger Cub in a big way and several more orders were placed, bringing 64 buses with Willowbrook or Park Royal bodies between 1956 and 1959. All further 1950s coaches were also Tiger Cubs: another eight from Willowbrook in 1955, this time with conventional front entrances, seven with classic Burlingham Seagull bodies in 1957 — the first from the Blackpool builder since before the war — and six in 1959 with the first of many bodies from Plaxton of Scarborough.

Beadle was the only supplier to break Leyland's monopoly of 1950s deliveries, and after the coaches two Chatham buses were supplied in 1955/6. Instead of employing used components the Chathams were all-new and featured Commer three-cylinder two-stroke diesel engines, reputedly developed by Tilling-Stevens (by now in the Rootes Group along with Beadle and Commer) from a German U-boat design! Although competent enough they were thoroughly out of place and were last used in 1963/4.

Another oddity was 676 (HE 9530) — a prewar coach created in 1952! It had a wonderfully complex career: the TS8 chassis was one of 30 with ECW bodywork delivered in 1940, but from 1947 it operated with a Roe body taken from a 1934 Lion. After 12 years of bus use 676 became a coach, with a 1938 Burlingham body bought originally to rebody a 1932 TS4 acquired from Pride of the Road in 1935. In this form 676 ran for Tracky from 1952 to 1957, and is seen alongside the railway arches in Barnsley bus station. *Author's collection; source unknown*

The first Tiger Cubs, delivered in 1954, included 24 buses with attractive 44-seat bodies built on the Isle of Anglesey by Saunders-Roe. Nos 1002-25 were further distinguished by matching registrations GHE 2-25. No 1015 is seen heading west from Huddersfield along Wakefield Road, which was used by all Tracky and County Motors services serving the town, pursued by Titan 836 (BHE 766). Both are heading for Barnsley, the Tiger Cub on service 33A via Denby Dale and Penistone, and the Titan on service 15 via Clayton West and Darton. Their routes would split at Dean Bottom, the Titan turning left to climb into Kirkburton, the single-decker heading south to Shepley. *A. B. Cross*

The Willowbrook-bodied Tiger Cubs of
1955 (1029-36) had bodywork of similar
outline to the 1954 coaches but with the
entrance at the front. The side mouldings
gave a more 'coach like' appearance and a
different style of fleetname was used,
'YTC' appearing in separate, bold capitals.
No 1036 (HHE 187) is seen here at
Waterdale, Doncaster, on 22 June 1963,
taking a break on a Birmingham–Bradford
journey. Behind is a West Yorkshire Road
Car Bristol LS dual-purpose vehicle, also
on Yorkshire Services work. Nos 1029-36
would be taken out of service in 1966,
the replacement Leopards being able to
lap up the motorway miles in a manner
impossible for a Tiger Cub. *Roger Holmes*

The quest for lightweight single-deckers led
to the appearance in 1955/6 of two alloy-
framed Beadle Chathams from the Rootes
Group, better known as the manufacturer
of Hillman cars! First to arrive was 1037
(HHE 188), which on 9 May 1959 was
about to leave Barnsley for Manchester.
The Beadles' Commer TS3 two-stroke
engines were noisy and not renowned for
their hill-climbing ability, yet Tracky was
obviously comfortable sending 1037 on an
arduous run via Woodhead. High above
it is an ex-LMS Ivatt 2-6-0 locomotive,
probably about to haul a stopping train from
Court House station to Sheffield. *John Kaye*

With a fine backdrop of South Pennine scenery the second Beadle Chatham, 1073 (LHE 141), heads for Southport on a seasonal express service. In the mid-1960s the journey from Doncaster to Southport was scheduled for 5 hours 22 minutes, and the last picking-up point was at Elland, with over three hours still to go. It was hard work for driver and passengers alike; in the 21st century holidaymakers would be flying from Doncaster's Robin Hood airport to Greece in considerably less time! *John Fozard*

▲ The brief flirtation with Beadle-Commers came to nothing, and Beadle closed down anyway, so more Tiger Cub buses were bought, the 1956 batch (1059-70) having Willowbrook bodies. No 1066 (JHE 843) is seen threading through the stalls of Barnsley's famous market in May Day Green, with the Cross Keys (demolished in the early 1970s) in the background. It is operating service 27 to Rotherham via Wentworth, on which Rotherham Corporation Transport ran alternate journeys (the only proper municipal buses seen in Barnsley); when this photograph was taken RCT's vehicle would probably have been an AEC Reliance, but between 1938 and 1951 RCT favoured the Bristol L for single-deck work, buying no fewer than 60 with centre-entrance bodies by Bruce, Cravens and East Lancs. *Author's collection; source unknown*

▲ Seven Tiger Cubs with Burlingham Seagull coachwork (1074-80) arrived in 1957. They were seen right across the company's express-service network, and 1074 (LHE 502), in a slightly revised livery with red lower front panel, is pictured at the Coliseum Coach Station in Blackpool. Tracky had a financial stake in Blackpool Omnibus Stations Ltd, which ran the Coliseum. In this August 1961 view 1074 had worked service J7 from Doncaster, Barnsley and Huddersfield (the 'J' prefix alluded to the joint services instigated in 1935 and surviving until the advent of the National Express numbering scheme in 1973). The Seagulls lasted until the late 1960s, but there were another six Tiger Cubs with very different-looking Seagull 70 bodies in 1961. *John Fozard*

Also in 1957 came 12 Willowbrook-bodied Tiger Cub buses (1093-1104), some at least arriving in cream and red. No 1099 (LHE 527) is seen on 19 October of that year, at Lower Mosley Street, Manchester, having operated service 20 from Barnsley via Penistone, Woodhead and Stalybridge; it would return the same way. The destination blinds were often set like this; showing both ends of a route avoided the need to reset them after each journey. *John Kaye*

A batch of 23 Tiger Cubs (1105-27) supplied in 1958 had the only single-deck bodies ever bought by Tracky from Park Royal. No 1121 (NHE 128) was freshly into service and utterly spotless in its mainly cream livery when seen at Waterdale on 20 May of that year. Despite its coach-style livery it is about to perform a mundane trip through the heart of industrial south Yorkshire, to Barnsley via Mexborough; the busy 22A service regularly employed single-deckers as duplicates to double-deckers. *Roger Holmes*

The passenger growth of the previous 50 years peaked in 1955 and was followed by a long and gradual decline, hastened by the Suez crisis of 1956 and a national busmen's strike in 1958. As the standard of living rose, private motoring became more affordable, while other social changes, notably the growing popularity of television, led to tough times for cinemas and fewer evening journeys. Even so, Tracky continued to be highly profitable, the fleet was constantly updated, and the route network remained stable; the few changes that were made were mostly to serve new or developing housing estates. The downside was that costs were also rising fast, and after 40 years of operation fares had to go up; until now profitability had been achieved simply by carrying vast numbers of passengers at very low fares.

By the middle of the decade the postwar Tigers had become a problem; some needed expensive structural attention to bodywork, and, with only 32 or 34 seats, they were of limited use. The clue to the solution lay in 722, the double-deck Tiger TS8, and refurbished PS1s formed the basis of the next double-deck type. In 1955 six 1947 chassis had their Weymann bodies removed and were thoroughly overhauled before returning to service with new highbridge Roe bodies and new registrations. A further 27 were converted in 1956/7, taken from the Roe- and Weymann-bodied vehicles of 1947 and the 1949 Brush-bodied batch. The old bodies were sold, some after as little as seven years' use, although one Weymann body was transferred to a 1949 chassis. Two other 1956 PS1 rebuilds were given lowbridge bodies, again by Roe; they had been intended for County Motors, in which fleet they originally had Roe single-deck bodies, but because of a disagreement with the licensing authorities in Huddersfield over whether they were genuinely new vehicles County lost out and ended up instead with two Guy utilities from Tracky.

The next double-deckers, built to the new maximum permitted length of 30ft, represented a technological leap forward, being rear-engined Leyland Atlanteans. Twelve — 73-seaters with low-height bodies by Weymann — were introduced in December 1959 on the services from Doncaster to Barnsley and Kilnhurst, which followed a common route as far as Swinton. In hindsight it seems scarcely credible that only nine years separated these modern buses from the Lancet saloons of 1950.

In the late 1950s many older double-deckers were withdrawn, including the remaining TD-series Titans, 722 (the Tiger which masqueraded as a Titan), the Foden and the Guys which retained their utility bodies. The decade closed with a fleet transformed, in which every vehicle had been bought new and almost half were of modern frontal appearance — a far cry from 1950, when the entire fleet had been of half-cab layout with exposed radiators.

◄

The Stocksbridge circular service (84) was a superb round-trip of an hour and 40 minutes from Barnsley and took in some very attractive countryside as well as the industrialised Upper Don Valley around Stocksbridge. Its anti-clockwise counterpart was the Langsett circular, numbered 81, both services running hourly. Tiger Cub 1126 (NHE 133), in dual-purpose livery, is just 14 minutes into its journey as it turns right at Stainborough crossroads to tackle the fearsome gradient of Stainborough Low towards Hood Green. *A. B. Cross*

In standard (red) bus livery but engaged on express work, for which cream would have been more appropriate, 1114 (NHE 121) is seen dropping passengers in Barnsley bus station. Instead of a service number the blinds are set to show 'EX PR ESS', and a paper windscreen sticker reveals that 1114 was operating on hire to North Western, technically the joint operator of the Barnsley–Manchester services. After its Tracky days were over, in 1972, 1114 was exported 'down under' by Paul Sykes, the renowned Barnsley bus dealer and entrepreneur (whose later claim to fame was the Meadowhall shopping centre in Sheffield), and found its way to an operator in Sydney! *S. J. Butler collection*

Six 1947 Tigers were rebodied by Roe as double-deckers in early 1955, re-emerging as 1038-43. No 1041 (HHE 322) stands gleaming at Chester Street bus station in Bradford, before operating the 2¾-hour journey to Dewsbury, Barnsley and Sheffield on service 66, which was shared with Yorkshire Woollen and SJOC; a Tracky bus would appear at Chester Street alternately at two- and four-hour intervals. Only an insider (or an enthusiast) could have known that 1041 had a previous life as 1947 Weymann-bodied PS1 single-decker 735 (AHE 466). To the right is JUM 378, a Titan PD1 from the renowned Samuel Ledgard of Armley fleet; it is bound for Leeds and what looks at first glance to be its destination display is in fact the information board for stand 19!
Author's collection; source unknown

There were only two lowbridge Tiger rebuilds (1071/2), originally intended for County Motors and based on two of its Roe-bodied PS1s. The new Roe-bodied double-deckers were prepared in County livery, but the licensing authorities in Huddersfield refused to accept them as new vehicles. In a fit of pique it was decided that they should be repainted red and diverted to Tracky, which was confident that the County Borough of Barnsley would allocate new registrations. County Motors (and passengers in Huddersfield) were the losers. The pair was usually based at Shafton, and 1072 (KHE 650) is seen in February 1957 outside South Yorkshire Motors' Ford showroom in Beastfair, Pontefract, having operated service 45 from Barnsley.
John Fozard

The Roe-bodied Titan TD5s of 1937-9 had very long lives, lasting until at least 1955. No 582 (HE 8235) of 1937 was a real stalwart, not being scrapped until the early months of 1957, and was already the last survivor of its batch when this photograph was taken on 5 August 1956. Few of the 54 seats are taken as it leaves Barnsley bus station and turns onto the wet cobblestones of Exchange station approach, heading for Gawber (Beever Lane) via Huddersfield Road on service 87. *John Kaye*

During the 1950s the independents brought a fascinating array of exotic vehicles to Barnsley bus station, at least six of them running double-deckers. The partners in the Ideal service, which operated to Pontefract, emulated Tracky in having PS1 Tigers rebodied as double-deckers, in each case losing a Wilkes & Meade coach body in favour of a new Roe lowbridge body. Wray's AHE 987 was treated in 1956, becoming KHE 526 in its new guise, and in its red-and-cream livery it could easily have passed for a Tracky bus. Taylor's FWX 932 followed in 1959, and, being based up the road in Cudworth, received West Riding registration YWT 572. For comparison, Tracky's highbridge equivalent 1057 (JHE 834) stands on the left — surely Tracky had a hand somewhere in these conversions? *A. P. Tatt Archive*

Tommy Burrows' Rawmarsh–Leeds service was one of the busiest independent services in the area until taken over by Tracky and West Riding in 1966. Burrows' first double-deckers — two Bristol Ks delivered in 1945 — were followed by new and second-hand AEC Regents. The first used examples were four with Roe bodies from Leeds City Transport in 1951, including Burrows' 73 (ANW 696), which dated from 1934 and lasted until 1957. Double-deckers often ran in pairs, and in this Barnsley bus station view the blinds confirm that 73 is serving as a duplicate. Burrows' buses regularly featured advertising for Clarksons' brewery, situated off Park Road in Barnsley, which was taken over by Tennants of Sheffield in the late 1950s. *Roy Marshall*

The final double-deck PS1 conversions (1081-92) came in 1957 and employed the chassis of various buses dating from the years 1947-9; 1087 (LHE 515) was formerly Brush-bodied 783 (BHE 444). In an all-too-rare Barnsley street scene it is seen at Town End, heading through the six-way junction on its way to Dodworth on service 40. Amongst the traffic following along Peel Street is a British Railways Scammell Scarab three-wheeler. Wrights' dispensary stood in the apex of Peel Street and Shambles Street, while diagonally opposite, at the bottom of Racecourse Road, was the much-lamented Wheatsheaf public house, which dispensed a fine pint of Tetley's; the junction is now a roundabout. *R. H. G. Simpson*

Only eight Guy Arab 'utilities' continued in service beyond 1952 with their original bodies, providing a stark reminder of the war years, and the last were withdrawn in 1959. Roe-bodied 716 (HE 9889) looked remarkably presentable when photographed in Barnsley bus station on 9 May of that year but would be sold for scrap seven months later. Already well loaded for its journey to Shafton Green via Stairfoot on service 90, it demonstrates just how cramped the upper deck of a lowbridge double-decker could get, with just an offside gangway. In the background are a Burlingham Seagull-bodied coach and a Tiger Cub/Park Royal bus in cream livery on service 11 to Doncaster via Grimethorpe. *John Kaye*

No 713 (HE 9866) illustrates the dramatic transformation achieved when Roe rebodied six 1944 Guy Arabs with new highbridge bodies in 1952, all six having originally had utility Weymann bodies, also of highbridge layout. It looks very well presented as it stands in Barnsley bus station on 8 September 1959, ready for the short run to Strafford Avenue at Ward Green, but would be scrapped three years later, along with the rest of the batch. *Roger Holmes*

Among the vehicles withdrawn at the end of the 1950s was 722 (HE 9542), which had started life in 1940 as 688, an ECW-bodied Tiger TS8. However, as it returned from Sheffield to Wombwell one evening in May 1944 it left the road near Harley and overturned in a wheat field, wrecking the bodywork. The chassis was then fitted with the Short body from the 1932 Daimler CP6 double-decker, being renumbered as 722, and in 1949 it was rebodied again, with the new Roe lowbridge body shown here, lasting in this form until 1959. It is seen on layover at Waterdale on 11 April of that year, before a journey on service 50C (since the 1935 co-ordination agreement licensed jointly with Doncaster Corporation Transport) from North Bridge to Skellow via Bentley. *Roger Holmes*

Thirty-three PS1s were rebodied as double-deckers between 1955 and 1957, but withdrawal of the others began in 1958. Brush-bodied 782 (BHE 443) completed its 11-year stint in 1960, when it was sold to North's of Leeds, subsequently being scrapped. On 24 April 1957 it was parked out of service at Waterdale, Doncaster, the destination showing 'PRIVATE' but the number blind implying use on service 21A. The paper advertisement in the foremost side window of the saloon reads: 'WANTED: 25 PSV DRIVERS'. *Roger Holmes*

The Dennis Lancets lasted in service until 1961/2, and on 9 May 1959 868 (CHE 360) is seen in Barnsley bus station, with the blind indicating a journey to Silkstone Common. For many years service 82 ran only on Saturdays, when the legendary Barnsley market created huge demand. The timetable was curious, an hourly service to Penistone being supplemented by short workings every hour and a half to Silkstone Common, where they turned at the Station Inn. The black smoke above the stands in the background reveals activity at Exchange station. *John Kaye*

The 1950s closed with the arrival of Tracky's first rear-engined vehicles, a batch of Weymann-bodied Leyland Atlanteans numbered 1151-62. They were real giants, with 73 seats (10 more than any previous double-deckers), in a lowbridge configuration with a nearside gangway at the rear of the upper saloon. No 1151 (RHE 801) shows its 'L' (for lowbridge) suffix as it crosses the Dearne & Dove Canal at Swinton Bridge before ducking down under the parallel railway line by Swinton station, where M&S's trolleybus wires prevented full-height buses from passing, on its way from Doncaster to Kilnhurst on service 24. No 1151 did well to survive until 1976, latterly numbered 600. *A. B. Cross*

Tracky's last PD2s were Nos 987-91, which entered service in 1953/4. They had highbridge Roe bodies with particularly deep lower-deck windows and for many years were favourites for the long jointly operated routes from Sheffield and Barnsley to Leeds and Bradford. No 988 (EHE 935) is seen leaving Wakefield bus station for Sheffield in July 1959, with a variety of West Riding buses in the background. A full round trip on service 67 took five hours, and the hourly service was generally maintained by two buses each from Tracky and West Riding and one from the Sheffield Joint Committee; however, in order to balance the mileage West Riding put out three buses on Wednesdays and Thursdays, reducing the Tracky requirement to one. *Bruce Jenkins*

The 1959 Tiger Cub buses (1128-44) had BET-style Willowbrook bodywork. When photographed in April 1962 1135 (OHE 708) was in bus livery but still considered suitable for excursions; it is shown in Kettlewell in Upper Wharfedale, heading south along the B6160 towards Grassington, and in another three miles would pass the famous Kilnsey Crag. This may have been Easter Monday, when Tracky advertised a Yorkshire Dales tour from Barnsley with stops at Leyburn, Aysgarth Falls, Grassington and Bolton Abbey; the adult fare was 12s 3d. After a relatively short career 1135 (469 from 1967) was withdrawn in 1970 and found its way to Glynn's Coaches of Graiguenaspidogue, in County Carlow in the Irish Republic. *John Fozard*

Between 1954 and 1962 Tracky took delivery of 30 Tiger Cub coaches, with bodies by Burlingham, Willowbrook and Plaxton. The 1959 batch (1145-50) had Plaxton Consort bodies and were the first of many coaches supplied to Tracky by the Scarborough builder, which from the mid-1960s until 2005 supplied the vast majority of Tracky's coaches. Here, 1147 (OHE 720) heads an amazing line-up, with a Tracky Burlingham Seagull immediately behind. Surprisingly, two of this batch would be among the first Tracky vehicles converted for one-man operation, for use on the Manchester services. *Author's collection; source unknown*

▲ When this photograph was taken in Sprotbrough village on 13 May 1961 the 1950 Tiger PS1s and Dennis Lancets were the last remaining half-cab single-deckers, and on their way out; both types would be eliminated in 1962. No 888 (CHE 722) is working Saturday-only service 48 from Thurnscoe, which had taken it from the heart of the industrial Dearne Valley through the attractive villages of Barnburgh and High Melton, and little over 10 minutes later journey's end would be reached in Doncaster. It is in the later livery with maroon (rather than black) wings. After sale 888 would become a works bus for McAlpine's in 1962. *Roger Holmes*

The PD2s put in sterling service well into the 1960s. On a beautiful July afternoon in 1962 Roe lowbridge bus 878 (CHE 609) leaves Grimethorpe along Engine Lane before continuing past its home depot at Shafton to Cudworth and Barnsley. Grimethorpe — *raison d'être* mining — manages to look almost rustic in this scene. No 878 had only three months' service left before passing to North's, the used-bus dealer, which would sell it on to an operator at Barton-on-Humber. Fewer than 10 of Tracky's 75 PD2s were to see further use with PSV operators, most being swiftly sold for scrap after reaching their 12th birthdays, when potentially expensive recertification would become necessary. *John Fozard*

5. The final years of BET

In 1961 five Tiger PS2s were rebodied with Roe double-deck bodies, re-entering service as 1190-4. No 1192 (VHE 192), which utilised the chassis of Windover-bodied coach 902 (CHE 857), is seen in Barnsley bus station after renumbering as 788, ready to depart for Yews Estate. In an attempt to overcome their top-heavy appearance these vehicles were subjected to various livery experiments, hence the broad cream band below the upper-deck windows. *Author's collection; source unknown*

They also reintroduced matching registrations, which were to feature on all subsequent deliveries until the County Borough of Barnsley ceased to be responsible for vehicle registration, in 1974. Five Roe-bodied buses — possibly the ugliest ever operated by Tracky — followed in 1961, and a final nine with Northern Counties bodies in 1963, based on the ex-Yorkshire Woollen chassis. At the same time five similar conversions, involving both Roe and Northern Counties bodywork, were undertaken by Tracky on behalf of Stratford Blue, a small BET company which lacked the engineering facilities to carry out such work itself.

By the end of 1960 the goal of an all-Leyland fleet was finally within sight, with sales of Lancet saloons and rebodied Guys due to begin. However, on 1 January 1961 the business of Camplejohn Bros of Darfield was acquired, bringing 10 vehicles of six different chassis makes — and not a Leyland among them! 'Camps' — from the same family as the Bentley operator acquired in 1935 — had run coaches and a Barnsley–Thurnscoe bus service. Amazingly, Tracky kept the service buses — an Atkinson and three Sentinels dating from 1952-5 — as well as a superb 1950 Dennis Lancet with Yeates body and a 1956 Plaxton-bodied Atkinson from the coach fleet. The newest coach, a Ford Thames Trader, passed to Mexborough & Swinton, while two Bedfords and a Commer were sold without being used.

By the start of the 1960s the downturn in passenger numbers was affecting almost all operators, but Tracky had less to worry about than most, and many routes still saw full buses, especially at peak times. Even so, the unbridled optimism of 10 years earlier had evaporated.

Following the success of the rebodied PS1s as budget-price double-deckers it was decided to convert the PS2s. All seven were withdrawn in 1960, eliminating the half-cab coach from the fleet, but by using two County Motors chassis and buying another nine from Yorkshire Woollen a class of 18 was built up by 1963. Nos 1186-9 (THE 186-9) entered service in the summer of 1960 sporting 63-seat Northern Counties bodywork and were Tracky's first front-engined double-deckers with forward entrances.

In the meantime the last Tiger Cubs were delivered, 23 buses with Metro-Cammell bodywork arriving in 1960/1 and the final six from Alexander in 1962 — the first time the Scottish builder

An eclectic selection of vehicles was acquired in January 1961 from Camplejohn Bros of Darfield. Six were taken into stock, numbered 129C-33C and 135C (134 having been used in 1949 for an ex-Hebble Titan, now long gone — someone had a good memory!). Camplejohns' 29 (LWT 880), one of two 1952 Sentinel STC6s with Sentinel engines and bodywork, became Tracky's 130C, lasting until 1963. It is seen here on 27 July 1961 at Glasgow Paddocks bus station, Doncaster (opposite Waterdale), working the busy service through Mexborough, Swinton and Wath to Barnsley, almost certainly duplicating a double-decker. *Roger Holmes*

An absolute gem from Camplejohns was 135C (JWT 842), a magnificent 1950 Dennis Lancet J3 with Yeates coachwork. At the time of acquisition it was Camplejohns' oldest coach, and Tracky's own half-cab coaches had already gone, but it was too good to discard and served Tracky for two seasons in this mainly red livery. It is seen here at Blackpool on express-service duty, immaculately turned out with a YTC monogram on the side. The 'C' suffix denoted a former Camplejohn vehicle, but there seemed little point to it, and later acquisitions from other operators had no letter suffix. *S. J. Butler collection*

There was yet more variety from the Camplejohns fleet in the shape of two unusual Gardner-engined Atkinsons — a bus and a coach. No 133C (XTD 665) had a Plaxton Venturer body and had been supplied new to Bracewells of Colne, Lancashire, in 1956, passing to 'Camps' in 1959. It lasted with Tracky until 1966 and is seen here carrying members of the Ryhill branch of the Wakefield Trinity (Rugby League) Supporters' Club.
Chris Orchard / Online Transport Archive

BET's approach to sourcing bodywork led to ample variety amongst Tracky's 117 Tiger Cub buses, Saunders-Roe, Willowbrook, Park Royal, Metro-Cammell and Alexander all having a share of the action. The 1960/1 Metro-Cammell buses (1163-85) included some in cream livery with coach-style script fleetnames. No 1183 (SHE 171) is seen in bus livery in St Sepulchre Gate, Doncaster, on 28 June 1964, embarking on the lengthy run to High Green on service 21. This would take in varied scenery, including rural Cadeby, High Melton and Adwick-on-Dearne, then industrial Mexborough, Manvers and Wath before striking west through Brampton, Elsecar and Hoyland to reach High Green Co-op after 88 minutes.
Roger Holmes

had supplied bodies to Tracky. The last coaches were six with Burlingham Seagull 70 coach bodies, delivered in 1961.

There was now a move to maximum-capacity vehicles, and 1961 brought 30ft-long Leyland PD3A/1s with 73-seat forward-entrance bodywork — the first Titans since the early 1950s. By 1965 there were 45, all bodied by Northern Counties apart from the final batch, which were the last Tracky buses with Roe bodies. Their sliding platform doors and fibre-glass fronts gave them a refreshingly modern appearance. The decision to revert to Titans probably says something about the reliability and operating costs of the early Atlanteans, but in low-height form the Atlantean did at least avoid the need for a full-length side gangway, and another six were delivered in 1964, with Weymann bodies little different from those supplied in 1959.

The operation of 36ft single-deckers was now permitted, and Leyland Leopards of this length proved ideal for bus and coach work. The first buses, in 1962, were seven Willowbrook-bodied 54-seaters (more seats than a lowbridge PD2!), and by the end of 1966 a further 36 had been taken into stock, these being 53-seaters with rather more attractive bodywork by Willowbrook, Marshall and Weymann.

Business on the London services was growing, encouraged by the opening of the M1 motorway, which took much of the Yorkshire–London traffic away from the A1, the historic Great North Road. Motorway operations demanded high-performance vehicles with increased passenger capacity, and three Leopard/Willowbrook 47-seat express coaches took to the road in early 1962. By the end of 1965 six more had arrived, of more modern but still bus-like appearance, to be joined the following year by a final example bodied by Weymann. This style of vehicle enjoyed brief popularity with several BET operators, and Willowbrook, keen to exploit the potential, exhibited Tracky Leopards at the Commercial Motor Shows of 1962 and 1964.

Another three Leopards delivered in 1962 had Plaxton Panorama coachwork. The Panorama design was perfect for tour and excursion work, and 15 of a revised style followed between 1965 and 1968, by which time it had also been adopted for express duties.

Two small coach operators were taken over in 1962 — Dan Smith of Darfield in March and Tom Roberts of Barnsley in August. Smith's 1954 Guy Arab UF with Burlingham Seagull body became Tracky's 136, but a Foden with a Windover body from a Tracky Tiger and a Leyland Comet were sold immediately. Roberts produced a 1955 Tiger Cub with Plaxton coachwork, which became Tracky's 137. Smith had also operated

a Darfield–Wombwell stage-carriage service, and Pickerill's was left as the final independent on this route until it too was swallowed up in January 1964, bringing a 1961 Duple-bodied Ford Thames and a similar Bedford SB of 1962, which survived for several years as Tracky 138 and 139.

Another independent service was taken over in 1965. Mosley's of Barugh Green had started the Barnsley–Higham service in the 1920s, and since the 1930 Road Traffic Act had had the road up to the village from Barugh Green to itself. From 1951 it used double-deckers, but it was apparently having difficulty in replacing its ex-Sheffield Daimler CWD6 and so decided to offer the service to Tracky, continuing in business as a coach operator.

After 26 years as General Manager Norman Dean retired in December 1965, bringing to a close a long and distinguished career; popular with the staff, he was a respected figure in the bus industry as well as locally, and in 1960 had been honoured with an OBE. His successor, Peter Wyke Smith, inherited a company in good shape but stayed only until 1968; for the next two decades no General Manager would last for more than five years, some staying for as little as two. Wyke Smith broke the tradition of general managers' residing at The Rookery, an old house on the Upper Sheffield Road site, which was now converted to accommodate the Traffic Department's offices.

A second batch of lowbridge Atlanteans (1270-5) arrived in 1964, looking little different from the 1959 buses. On 8 June of that year 1274 (3274 HE) turns into Barnsley bus station from Queens Road while busy on service 106, which served Athersley, but was operationally linked to the 102 to Park House Estate, better known today as Kendray. Athersley was a large area of postwar housing, and at the busiest times the 106 and 109, which traversed the estate in opposite directions, each ran every 15 minutes. No 1274, later renumbered 616, would last in service until 1980, when it was sold for scrap. *Iain MacGregor*

The first 36ft Leyland Leopards were three express coaches (1230-2) delivered early in 1962. Like the first Tiger Cubs for express work in the 1950s they had modified Willowbrook bus bodies, the most obvious alterations on the Leopards being the rather dated side mouldings (which did not suit the lines of the body), the positioning of the blinds below the windscreen and the narrow entrance. This view of 1230 (XHE 230), heading north to Barnsley, shows the rounded front dome with 'Motorway Express' lettering, expanded to 'Yorkshire–London Motorway Express' on the side. After seven years this vehicle (renumbered 200 in 1967) would become a 53-seat service bus (343), surviving until 1976. *R. H. G. Simpson*

Tracky's first Leopard buses (1233-9) were possibly the first 36ft Leopard buses to enter service anywhere in the country. They had 54-seat Willowbrook bodies and were capable of replacing older double-deckers on a one-for-one basis, but services 42/42A/42B to Ryhill and Newstead were always single-deck-operated because of the low bridge between Royston and Monckton Main Colliery. Under the 1967 scheme 1235 (XHE 235) was renumbered 302, in which guise it is seen turning into Barnsley bus station from Queens Road, after removal of the railway bridge leading to Court House station, which had lost its passenger services in April 1960. *Author's collection; source unknown*

No 1249 (YHE 249) was displayed by Willowbrook at the 1962 Commercial Motor Show as an example of the express-coach *genre*. The more angular bodywork style with curved windscreen glass was widely adopted by BET operators, and very similar-looking vehicles would be bought by Tracky for the next 10 years, mainly for bus use. Ready to return north, 1249 is seen at Victoria Coach Station on 8 August 1964 between a Midland Red C3 or C4 and an Eastern Counties Bristol MW, with a Black & White Motorways Leopard behind. *P. K. Mankelow*

Delivered at intervals from 1962 to 1981 were more than 40 Plaxton-bodied Leopard coaches, of which the first three (1252-4) had 49-seat Panorama bodies. Someone worked out that 1253 (1253 HE) was the 1,000th Leyland supplied to either Barnsley & District or Yorkshire Traction, and a handover ceremony was arranged to mark the event in Barnsley bus station. Norman Dean OBE, who by now had been General Manager for well over 20 years, is at the centre of the group on the right. The coach carried a small chrome '1000' insignia, just visible between the front grille and the Leyland Leopard badge. *Ian Allan Library*

This 1955 Plaxton-bodied Tiger Cub, 137 (HHE 200), came with Tom Roberts' coach business in 1962 and served Tracky until 1966. It is seen here in Barnsley bus station, about to venture westwards across the Pennines to Manchester, on either service 19 via Holmfirth and the Isle of Skye or the 20 via Penistone and Woodhead. Either way, it should have been at Lower Mosley Street in a little under two hours, provided there were no abnormal weather conditions. In 1972 Tracky's single fare from Barnsley to Manchester was 35p, with a day-return fare of 50p; nowadays it costs more than that to ride from one bus stop to the next! *Peter Roberts*

Another of the many oddities placed in service from acquired operators during the 1960s was 136 (NDA 14), a Burlingham Seagull-bodied Guy Arab UF of 1954, inherited in March 1962 from Dan Smith of Darfield. Its Wolverhampton registration was due to its original operator, Don Everall, rather than to Guy Motors, which was also based in the town. Tracky would run the Guy — which at first glance looked similar to the 1957 Tiger Cubs but in fact had an earlier and purer version of the classic Seagull body — until 1965. In this busy Saturday-morning scene at Waterdale it is bound for Bridlington. *Richard Simons*

The 8ft-wide Titan PD2/12s of 1951-3 all lasted until at least 1967. No 943 (DHE 795), with Leyland's own lowbridge bodywork, went just before the 1967 renumbering and is pictured here in later years, looking very smart with maroon wings; clearly visible is the oval Yorkshire Traction radiator badge which Tracky affixed to many Tigers and Titans in place of the usual 'Leyland'. The bus is seen at Stand 15 in Barnsley bus station, prior to departure for Kexbrough. *Peter Roberts*

No 943 again, in an interesting encounter in Pontefract bus station which illustrates the difference between the PD2/12 Titans and the shorter and narrower PD2/1s whilst providing further evidence of the co-operation which existed between Tracky and some of the Pontefract Road operators. Both were 1951 buses with lowbridge Leyland bodies and had reached Pontefract from Barnsley via Hemsworth. No 943 (DHE 795) is working service 45 via Ackworth, operated jointly with South Yorkshire Motors, while the former 935 (DHE 573), which had been sold in 1964 to Wray of Hoyle Mill, is on the hourly Ideal service via Upton, shared with Taylor of Cudworth. Taylor's operations would pass to Tracky in 1967, and Wray's in 1974. *S.J. Butler collection*

Norman Dean had promised that every possible economy would be pursued before any service cuts were implemented, so one-man operation became a necessity. The Manchester services were converted first, in July 1966, and among the vehicles modified were two Tiger Cub/Plaxton coaches. From this small beginning OMO spread to many single-deck duties and later to double-deckers, and within 20 years the role of conductor would be completely eliminated.

The 1965 Titans were the last front-engined double-deckers. Atlanteans with 75-seat Northern Counties bodies were bought each year from 1966 to 1968, and design improvements meant that a central upstairs gangway was now achievable within a low-height bus.

In terms of styling they represented a considerable improvement over the original Atlanteans, and those delivered from 1967 had extra-long 'panoramic' side windows. Significantly, in 1968 an equivalent number of Daimler Fleetlines was bought, with similar bodywork — the first Daimlers for more than 30 years and the first Gardner-engined buses since the war.

The most notable acquisition of the 1960s was of the long-established Rawmarsh–Barnsley–Wakefield–Leeds route (at around 40 miles said to be Yorkshire's longest independent stage-carriage service) of 'Tommy' Burrows & Sons of Wombwell, taken over in October 1966. Burrows' 12 AEC-engined double-deckers were acquired, but they all were at least 10 years old and were sold *en bloc* to a dealer without being used; among them were eight AEC Regents, ranging from a 1946 Mk II to a 1956 Mk V, a wartime Bristol K and three ex-London Transport Daimlers of similar vintage, the oldest six, dating from 1947 or earlier, having been rebodied in the late 1950s. The purchase was made jointly with West Riding, which played only a very small part in the operation of what became service 99. Burrows continued in business, running contract services with coaches and single-deckers. Six months later Robert Taylor's share of the Ideal service from Barnsley to Pontefract was taken over, but without any of his all-Leyland fleet.

At around this time many BET companies were subtly modernising their image, with more contemporary fleetname styles and, sometimes, minor adjustments to the livery. Tracky did the same, adopting a fleetname with capital letters of equal height with no underlining and fleet numbers of similar style. Traditional red and cream was retained, but the practice of painting wings maroon ceased, this now being considered an unnecessary cost.

Up to this point all new vehicles since 1913 (and most of those acquired second-hand) had been numbered sequentially, the 1966 Atlanteans finishing at 1343 (FHE 343D). This system did not help the depot staff, who had to ensure that vehicles were correctly allocated; sending 1243 (a double-decker) to Penistone

instead of 1234 could have had disastrous consequences! Early in 1967, coinciding with introduction of the new image, the fleet was renumbered, using a 'block' system. This employed separate series for lowbridge and full-height double-deckers and allowed the 'L' and 'H' suffixes to be discontinued, but it was mainly after the disappearance of conductors that some unfortunate mishaps involving low bridges occurred; clearly something beyond a new numbering system was needed!

The first vehicles delivered with the new numbers were Leopard coaches 15/16 (JHE 615/6E), earlier examples having been renumbered 1-14. Further new Leopards included 12 dual-purpose vehicles with Marshall bodywork in 1967 and three with Alexander Y-type bodies — the first of many of this style — in 1968, together with seven short 45-seaters from Marshall.

BET had been an outspoken critic of nationalisation, but in March 1968 it voluntarily sold its UK bus-operating interests to the state, which placed them with the former British Transport Commission shareholdings in the hands of the Transport Holding Company. Tracky was now fully state-owned, and a hint of the extensive changes ahead came in October, when County Motors was placed under its wing; within three months Tracky was part of the newly formed National Bus Company, and County was gone.

The last buses delivered with fleet numbers in the original series were 10 PDR1/2 Atlanteans, with 75-seat Northern Counties bodywork, which arrived in 1966 as 1334-43. In this busy scene in Barnsley bus station 1335 (FHE 335D) shows Moorland Avenue (Staincross) as its destination, although the 76 was the service to Darfield Road at Cudworth. Alongside is 1201 (VHE 201), a 1961 Titan PD3 (also with Northern Counties body), which had apparently just arrived from Holmfirth on the infrequent 38 via Denby Dale and Kexbrough. *Peter Roberts*

Under the 1967 renumbering lowbridge double-deckers were numbered in the 600-99 range, and 977 (EHE 924), a 1953 PD2/12 with Northern Counties body, became 693, surviving in service until 1969. It is seen early in 1968 in unfamiliar territory, arriving at Halifax bus station on Hebble Motor Services' 17 service from Bradford via Queensbury. Hebble had a need for lighter double-deckers because of a temporary weight restriction, and Tracky obliged with four PD2s, receiving four 71-seat AEC Regent Vs in return. Coincidentally Tracky started operating into Halifax in its own right on 1 April 1968, when certain journeys on the Sheffield–Huddersfield service (68) were extended to Halifax as X68s. In the background a Hebble AEC Reliance waits to leave for Rochdale via Ripponden on service 28. *John Fozard*

The last of four batches delivered from 1961, the 10 Titan PD3s (1306-15) of 1965 were notable in several respects: as well as being the last Roe-bodied buses ever supplied to Tracky they were the last front-engined vehicles to be delivered and were destined to be the last to be withdrawn, in 1977, after 47 years' continuous operation of Leyland Titans. Formerly 1313, 742 (CHE 313C) is seen immediately after leaving Wakefield bus station, engaged on service 65 from Leeds to Sheffield; 37 minutes later, after travelling via Newmillerdam and Staincross, it would reach Barnsley. Note the recruitment advertisement for the National Coal Board. *John May*

In May 1967 the 'South West Clipper' services began operation, creating another complex multi-operator 'pool'. Tracky vehicles then became an increasingly familiar sight in the West Country, and Cheltenham coach station is the setting for these Marshall-bodied dual-purpose Leopards from the 1967 batch (210-21). These vehicles could be seen across the whole spectrum of Tracky's activities, operating express services, excursions and limited-stop and local stage-carriage services. Nos 217 and 221 (JHE 517/21E) would be withdrawn in 1979, having operated latterly in NBC liveries. *PM Photography*

This view at Upper Sheffield Road demonstrates the importance to Tracky of colliery services, with buses due to leave for the early-afternoon shift changes. Heading for Barrow Colliery is 1957 Willowbrook-bodied Tiger Cub 431 (LHE 525), while 1963 PS2 rebuild 797 (YHE 246) will run to Woolley. This was one of Tracky's last new buses with traditional exposed radiators, nine Northern Counties 63-seaters on rebuilt Tiger PS2 chassis (1240-8, later renumbered 791-9). The chassis for these came from Yorkshire Woollen, and that of 797 had originally formed the basis of YW 712 (HD 8566). Barrow Colliery, incidentally, was at Worsbrough and not (as the author wrongly assumed in his early days in Barnsley) at Barugh — which is pronounced 'Bark'. *Photobus*

6. County Motors

In the early postwar period 10 single-deck bodies were ordered from Roe and fitted in 1948/9 to six PS1s (73-8) and four PS2s (83-6). No 83 (EVH 211) stands in Waterloo depot yard, looking typically immaculate in County's postwar ivory and blue; this was one of the brightest bus liveries in the area, not unlike Sheffield Corporation's, except that the blue was a lighter shade. Following withdrawal in 1960 this vehicle would re-emerge as a Tracky double-decker, with forward-entrance Roe bodywork, numbered 1193 (VHE 193).
Peter Roberts

County Motors (Lepton) Ltd had been one of Yorkshire's most distinctive bus operators, and its loss was particularly sad.

Its origins were typical enough: the company was registered in 1919, soon after A. and B. Farrar started running buses from Huddersfield to Lepton, Flockton and Emley, and by 1923 the 'County Bus Service' reached Dewsbury and Wakefield. However, in 1927 the owners offered the business for sale, and the outcome was what made County unique: the three major neighbouring operators — Barnsley & District, West Riding and Yorkshire Woollen — made a successful joint bid, the two BET operators and independent West Riding each acquiring a one-third stake. By 1925 the operating base had moved to Waterloo, remaining there (rather than at Lepton) until the end.

The new owners inherited 18 buses, all AECs or REOs bodied by Taylor of Barnsley, and none more than two years old. To replace them they chose buses which conformed more closely with their own fleets, and initially this meant Leylands. Lions were bought from 1928 to 1934, while a lone ADC, which had originated with Aston of Jump, was transferred from Yorkshire Traction in 1930. At the start of 1935 the fleet was composed exclusively of Lions, but by 1939 16 Roe-bodied Tigers had been delivered.

Wartime pressures led to the first double-deckers, nine 'utility' Guy Arabs, most with lowbridge bodywork by Roe, but including two with highbridge Park Royal bodies. More double-deckers came after the war, starting in 1949 with four Guy Arab IIIs with lowbridge Roe bodies for the Dewsbury and Wakefield services via Scissett. The services to Barnsley and to Wakefield via Flockton were free of height restrictions, and to operate these County bought four highbridge Leyland Titans: two Leyland-

bodied PD2/3s in 1950 and two PD2/12s with Roe bodywork in 1952. Roe-bodied Tigers were chosen again for single-deck work, six PS1s and four PS2s arriving in 1948/9.

In place of the previous mainly blue scheme, postwar vehicles wore an attractive livery of ivory with a blue roof and three blue bands on double-deckers and one on single-deckers. In the 1960s this was amended so that double-deckers had only one blue band, losing only a little of its panache.

County generally had a modern fleet, and the last prewar buses went in 1950. As with Tracky, rebodying was pursued in the early 1950s, five utility Guys receiving new Roe bodies. Four postwar Tigers were also rebodied, starting in 1954 with two PS2s, which, although only five years old, received new

Guy Arab 69 (CCX 797) of 1945, still with original 'utility' lowbridge body, and 1948 Tiger PS1 78 (DVH 757), stand side by side in Huddersfield, on a patch of land used for bus parking pending redevelopment. Both have Roe bodies, County's standard choice from 1933. The photograph dates from April 1952, and within four years both vehicles would be fitted with new lowbridge double-deck bodies by the same builder, the Guy in 1953 and the Tiger in 1956, but instead of running for County as intended the latter would become Tracky's 1072 (KHE 650). *John Fozard*

In 1953 three of County's nine wartime Guy Arabs received new lowbridge bodies — by Roe, of course. On one of the routes requiring lowbridge double-deckers, 69 (CCX 797) looks a fine sight with its replacement body as it leaves Dewsbury in 1959, on its way to Huddersfield via Mirfield and Kirkheaton; compare this with the 1952 picture of the same bus on the left. All the Guys had six-cylinder engines, essential for tackling some of the tough gradients on County's routes, such as the long drag from Waterloo up Wakefield Road to Lepton and on to Emley Moor. *John Fozard*

In County's superb livery almost anything could look smart, including ex-Tracky utility Guy Arab 75 (HE 9917), the unexpected and unwanted substitute for a newly rebodied Tiger PS1. This photograph, taken in Wakefield bus station on 19 April 1957, illustrates the delights of open rear platforms as the lady passenger follows the children off the bus after its run from Huddersfield via Scissett. In the background is West Riding's lowbridge PD2 757 (GHL 306). *John Cockshott archive*

Windover bodies — the only coaches County ever had. A year later two PS1s were withdrawn for conversion to double-deckers, but, as related earlier, these ended up with Yorkshire Traction, and County instead gained its first second-hand vehicles for 25 years — two wartime Tracky Guys. These and the other remaining utilities were replaced in 1958 by four Guy Arab IVs, again with lowbridge bodywork by Roe.

The first new single-deckers for 10 years were Tiger Cubs, as favoured by Tracky. The 1959 pair had Willowbrook bodies and a mainly blue livery, leading to speculation (incorrect, as it happens) that they were intended for BET's Stratford Blue subsidiary, while the 1960 pair had Metro-Cammell bodies. They replaced the last Tigers, one of which stayed local, being used by Baddeley Bros of Holmfirth on its services from Huddersfield to Deepcar and to Penistone.

A quirk of shared ownership was that postwar single-deckers generally followed Tracky practice, whereas double-deckers were influenced by West Riding, two Guy Wulfrunians delivered in 1961 providing the ultimate proof. West Riding had worked with Guy Motors in developing this infamous model, which contributed to the downfall of both. County kept its Wulfrunians for less than two years and, as if frightened off by technological advancement, chose thoroughly traditional Roe-bodied Titan PD3s as replacements. These were very much in the Tracky mould and were County's last double-deckers.

Of 24 vehicles at the end of 1961, 18 were double-deckers. However, the longer single-deckers now available could meet demand, and Leyland Leopards with BET-style bodywork were bought from 1962 to 1967, followed by two more Tiger Cubs

in 1967/8. The balance of the fleet was thus reversed in just six years, and now only six double-deckers remained.

County's services changed little over the years, linking Huddersfield with Barnsley, Dewsbury and Wakefield and sharing a common route as far as Waterloo. Despite their inter-urban role they had a very rural feel. By contrast, during the 1960s County also regularly operated on hire to Yorkshire Woollen on the main-road service to Dewsbury.

In 1967 West Riding, weakened by the 'Wulfrunian crisis', sold out to the state-owned Transport Holding Company, and when BET did likewise early in 1968 County's owners were finally in the same camp. County's separate existence no longer made sense, and from October the company was placed under Tracky control, and buses started to appear in red and cream. This proved to be just a short step on the way to full integration, which took effect from 1 January 1969, and under NBC all trace of County Motors quickly disappeared, ending half a century of tradition.

West Riding influence led to the appearance in 1961 of two Guy Wulfrunians, but within two years County had tired of their revolutionary features and despatched them to join others of the type with West Riding, which eventually amassed almost every Wulfrunian ever produced. The configuration was unique at the time for a double-decker, with a front engine *and* space for an entrance alongside the driver. No 100 (UCX 276) is seen in Lord Street, Huddersfield, during its short stint with County. The service to Wakefield via Flockton was the Wulfrunians' usual haunt, perhaps because West Riding's engineers would be on hand at their destination if the worst happened! Bringing up the rear is Tracky's 831 (BHE 761), a 1949 Titan, on service 80 to Kirkburton. *John Fozard*

No 102 (WVH 231), one of County's first pair of Leyland Leopards, delivered in 1962 with 54-seat Willowbrook bodywork, is seen at Grange Moor, with 1967 Tiger Cub 113 (KCX 263E) behind. The styling, especially the front trim, was reminiscent of the late 1950s, and subsequent Leopards had more angular but neater BET-style bodies, similar to the Marshall body on 113. No 102, as its informative destination blinds reveal, was on its way to Barnsley via Emley, Flockton and Darton, having already traversed Highgate Lane at Lepton, with a smartly uniformed conductress on the platform. *Geoff Lumb*

7. Mexborough & Swinton

Just nine months after the demise of County Motors, Tracky took over the Mexborough & Swinton Traction Co, spelling the end for another of Yorkshire's most interesting operators, celebrated above all for its single-deck trolleybuses, which ran for almost 50 years.

The company's origins were in many ways similar to Tracky's, and, like Barnsley & District, the Mexborough & Swinton Tramways Co was registered in 1902. The Mexborough tramway was more extensive, but while B&D expanded to run buses over a wide area M&S very much stuck to its roots. Its territory lay to the north of Rotherham, and its heart was the route to Denaby and, later, Conisbrough — this was south Yorkshire at its most industrial, dominated by mining and glass and steel works, but there were odd stretches of countryside and some picturesque spots around the castle in Conisbrough.

The tramway, owned by the National Electric Construction Co, opened in 1907 and ran from the Rotherham borough boundary through Swinton and Mexborough to the Old Toll Bar at Denaby, while its 20 double-deck cars were housed in a depot at Rawmarsh, a couple of miles north of Rotherham. Contact studs between the

rails were used for electricity supply, but this proved disastrously unreliable and led to several fires, explosions and electrocuted horses, so overhead wiring was installed during 1908. Operation over Corporation tracks to Rotherham town centre now began, and in return Corporation cars ran to Parkgate, joint operation continuing in various forms for the next 80 years.

Motor-bus operation was tried in 1910, using a Thornycroft borrowed from a Scottish NEC company, but did not resume until the 1920s. Instead trolleybuses were chosen, and services between Mexborough and Manvers Main and the Old Toll Bar and Conisbrough were instituted in August 1915. This was a pioneering move; trolleybuses were in their infancy and still regarded as 'trackless' or 'rail-less' tramcars rather than as electric buses. Britain's first trolleybus routes had commenced operation in Bradford and Leeds in 1911 (Rotherham following in 1912), and the M&S 'tracklesses' were the first in the country that were not municipally operated. The initial three Daimlers were joined by another from Stockport Corporation in 1917 and operated from a small depot at the Old Toll Bar. Unfortunately, due to technical problems, both services saw lengthy periods of suspension, but M&S kept faith with trolleybuses and bought three new AECs in the years 1922-4.

Regular motor-bus operation started in 1922, three Daimlers providing a Mexborough–Bolton-on-Dearne–Goldthorpe service. A Kilnhurst–Upper Haugh service using two Dennises followed in 1925, but the Goldthorpe service was handed over to Yorkshire Traction in 1929.

The AECs showed that trolleybuses were capable of replacing the trams, and authority for them to do so was given in 1927. The original trolleybus routes were then linked across Mexborough and extended to Brook Square ('Conisbrough Low') and Conanby ('Conisbrough High'), and the last trams, on the Swinton–Rotherham section, ran in March 1929.

The Conisbrough end of route C could hardly have been more different from the industrial nightmare of Manvers, less than four miles away. Here the same trolleybus, heading for the 'Conisbrough High' terminus at Conanby, turns sharply between ancient stone walls as it negotiates the steep and narrow roads beneath the keep of the Norman castle. After the closure of the M&S system 37 migrated to Bradford, where it received a new double-deck body and lasted until the very end of British trolleybus operation in 1972. This location has changed little, and First's Wright-bodied Volvo B9TL double-deckers now come this way on the high-frequency X78 service from Doncaster to Sheffield.
Geoff Lumb

A fleet of 27 single-deck Garretts replaced not only the trams but the earlier trolleybuses, another three coming in 1930, and under the joint arrangements Corporation trolleybuses now ran through to Mexborough and Conisbrough.

In 1931 National Electric Construction, M&S's parent company, sold out to BET, and M&S became a sister company of Yorkshire Traction. The first buses bought under BET were two 20-seat Dennises in 1933, but in 1935 a Leyland Lion was transferred from Tracky; these three made up the motor-bus fleet until 1939, when an ex-Hebble Albion and two Tracky Leyland Cubs replaced them, to be joined in 1941 by an Albion Victor, also from Tracky.

The trolleybus fleet was strengthened with six English Electrics from the Nottinghamshire & Derbyshire system in 1937 and five elderly Guys from BET's Hastings operation in 1942, six 'utility' Sunbeams following in 1943. After the war a green-and-cream livery replaced the original maroon, and between 1947 and 1950 33 new Brush-bodied Sunbeams ousted the last prewar trolleybuses.

The first motor vehicles added to the fleet after the war were Bedford OBs, a two-year-old bus coming from East Yorkshire to start a local service between Mexborough and Windhill in 1948. Five new Duple-bodied OBs followed, including three Vista coaches, but they (and the Windhill service) were gone by 1953. There followed further short-lived acquisitions from fellow BET subsidiaries, two Leyland Lions being received from Sheffield United Tours in 1950, and four 1939 AEC Regal saloons — the first diesel-engined vehicles — from Devon General in 1952.

M&S finally looked serious about conventional buses when 10 very BET Weymann-bodied Leyland Tiger Cubs arrived in 1954. Motor buses now entered Rotherham for the first time, on a new service from the Monkwood estate and in lieu of trolleybuses on the Green Lane route (this having been the last extension to the system, in 1934). A 1939 Leyland Tiger came from Maidstone & District in 1955 as a reserve. The Regals and the

utility trolleybuses were thus replaced, the trolleys being rebodied as double-deckers by Doncaster Corporation.

In 1955 a Tiger Cub with Burlingham Seagull coachwork arrived to launch a programme of excursions and tours, to be joined by another in 1958; both would be rather brutally converted for bus use after the arrival of newer coaches in the late 1960s.

Nine more Tiger Cub buses had arrived by 1960, some arousing national interest as Continental-style 'crush-loader' buses with only 32 seats but room for 29 standing. They had beefed-up chassis and bigger engines, as well as a longer front overhang for a wide entrance, and were used mainly on the service between Mexborough (Highwoods) and Conisbrough (Ellershaw), which extended to Manvers Main at shift times.

In the early 1950s it was decided not to extend the trolleybus system, and powers to close it were obtained in 1959. The Manvers–Conisbrough High service was converted to motor bus from 1 January 1961, while the final closure came on 26 March, when M&S's first double-deck buses — 11 Weymann-bodied Atlanteans similar to those supplied to Tracky in 1959 — replaced the Rotherham–Conisbrough Low trolleybuses, BET's last. Trolleybus No 29 was converted to open-top layout for the last day and traversed the route with a brass band playing.

Another three Atlanteans came in 1961/2 and between 1961 and 1965 were complemented by 11 former Southdown Titans, ranging from rebodied prewar TD5s to 1951 PD2/12s. Daimler Fleetlines followed, a lone Weymann-bodied example arriving in 1964 and 10 with Northern Counties bodywork in 1967/8. There were no more new single-deckers.

The coach fleet also benefited from Southdown's cast-offs, three Beadle-Leylands acquired in 1962 being followed by Royal Tigers with Leyland and Harrington bodies, while Tracky's only postwar transfer, in 1961, was the Thames Trader acquired from Camplejohns. Three new Duple-bodied Leyland Leopard coaches were received between 1965 and 1967, while Bedfords reappeared in the shape of three Harrington-bodied SB5s from Northern General. However, the oddest vehicles of the 1960s were two SBs with Yeates Pegasus bus bodywork which had previously run for independents and were bought from a dealer in 1968; M&S used them for quieter one-man duties.

From the mid-1960s many service developments demonstrated a closer relationship with Tracky. A Mexborough (Windhill)–Rotherham–Sheffield service was started in 1965, and a Rotherham–West Melton service in

In contrast to Yorkshire Traction, M&S only ever operated one Leyland Tiger, a 1939 TS8 with ECW 35-seat body acquired from Maidstone & District in 1955. No 90 (FKO 81) is seen positioned between two Tiger Cubs in Rawmarsh depot yard. The blinds are set for service S; whilst the trolleybus routes were simply lettered A, B and C, the motor-bus route letters gave a clue to the destination, such as K for Kilnhurst Road and S for Sandhill. After withdrawal in 1959 the Tiger made itself useful as a towing wagon until 1966. *Author's collection; source unknown*

Although M&S's first double-deck buses were the trolleybus-replacement Atlanteans, for a time in the 1960s its Rawmarsh depot was home to various ex-Southdown Titans, some of which even retained their previous operator's livery of apple green and cream. The first (and oldest) were two 1938/9 TD5s rebodied in 1950 by Northern Counties. No 15 (FCD 509) stands opposite the depot, driverless, as the relief conductress crosses Dale Road ready for the onward journey to Mexborough on service 8, formerly trolleybus route A. *Colin Routh*

It wasn't just double-deckers that came from Southdown; the Brighton company also proved a useful source of coaches, including four all-Leyland Royal Tigers which dated from 1952 and came north in 1963/4. No 107 (LUF 637) looks well in cream and green, with the full 'Mexborough & Swinton' fleetname, which was introduced when the trolleybuses were replaced. In the late 1960s the shorter 'Mexborough' version was favoured again, but the company's image was otherwise unmodified.
Peter Roberts

The first Daimler since the 1920s, 19 (CWY 319B) was a Weymann-bodied Fleetline bought in preference to further Atlanteans. The distinctive moulding on the front panels, as on the Atlanteans, was probably intended to replicate the 'V' shape on the front of the trolleybuses. Barely a month old, it was photographed on 15 October 1964 approaching Denaby Crossing from the direction of Mexborough, heading towards the rather enigmatic destination of Conisbrough 'W' on service 9A. This was the former trolleybus route B from Rotherham to Conisbrough Low.
Roger Holmes

1967; previously the lack of through buses between Wath and Rotherham had been a glaring omission, passengers having to change at 'The Woodman'. A jointly operated Conisbrough–Wath (Newhill) service began in 1968, M&S then closing the Old Toll Bar depot and concentrating all operations at Rawmarsh. There were also changes to the joint workings with Rotherham Corporation, which for a time operated on the Rawmarsh circulars instead of on the Mexborough and Conisbrough services.

M&S survived to become a free-standing National Bus Company subsidiary from January 1969, although Tracky provided some management support from 1968. However, this status lasted just nine months as NBC rationalised its Yorkshire businesses, and from the end of September M&S was officially absorbed by Tracky, which took over the Rawmarsh depot and 40 vehicles. The green buses were very quickly confined to history, and the future of Rawmarsh was red!

8. NBC — the early years

The National Bus Company came into being on 1 January 1969, taking over all the former BET and THC operators. Between them the two groups had had more subsidiaries in Yorkshire's West Riding than in any other county (County Motors, Hebble, Mexborough & Swinton, Sheffield United Tours, West Riding, West Yorkshire, Yorkshire Traction and Yorkshire Woollen). NBC also inherited the railway interests in the Joint Omnibus Committees — institutions unique to the West Riding — at Halifax, Huddersfield, Sheffield and Todmorden. Rationalisation was essential, and for Tracky it would mean expansion.

From day one County Motors ceased to exist. Tracky took on the Waterloo depot and County's 23 buses, which, apart from four Guy Arabs, were all Leylands. Tracky's own Huddersfield depot, in Lincoln Street, was then closed, and all operations from the town were centred on Waterloo, the ex-County routes to Dewsbury and Wakefield introducing Tracky buses to such unfamiliar locations as Emley, Flockton and Mirfield. Some County buses had already been repainted red during the last quarter of 1968, and the rest quickly followed, while the bus services were numbered, something County had never found necessary.

Nine months later Mexborough & Swinton was also consigned to history, its 40 vehicles and the depot at Rawmarsh passing to Tracky on 1 October 1969. Tracky now had a major presence in Rotherham for the first time, mainly on the intensive operations

to Rawmarsh and beyond to Mexborough and Conisbrough; for many years company buses had only entered Rotherham on service 27 from Barnsley via Wentworth, on which Rotherham Corporation ran alternate journeys, although there had been a service to Greasbrough until Corporation trolleybuses took over in 1936. Rotherham Corporation (and, later, South Yorkshire PTE) retained a minority involvement in some of the services taken over from M&S — a relic of tramway practice 60 years earlier. Fourteen Leyland Atlantean and seven Daimler Fleetline double-deckers were acquired, along with 11 Tiger Cubs, three Leopard coaches, and five Bedford SBs. Immediately after the takeover the Tracky fleet total briefly topped 400 — an all-time high.

County Motors' 23 buses passed into Tracky ownership in January 1969. The oldest and most endearing were four 1958 Roe-bodied Guy Arabs, reintroducing the type to Tracky after several years' absence. Not visible here are the platform doors, which had never featured on Tracky's own rear-entrance double-deckers. Because lowbridge buses were no longer needed at Huddersfield, the Guys were transferred to Barnsley, and 688 (NCX 179) is seen heading towards the bus station on the linked Worsbrough Common (4) and Dodworth (40) services (which also had no need of lowbridge buses!). Its career with Tracky was short; by August it was gone, and in October its number was reused on an ex-Mexborough & Swinton Atlantean.
Michael Fowler

No 594 (OVH 606) was a
Willowbrook-bodied Tiger Cub,
previously County Motors 95,
and late in 1968 had run in
Tracky livery with County
fleetnames. It is seen on 31 July
1969 leaving Dewsbury bus
station on the ex-County service
to Huddersfield via Mirfield,
the yellow triangle on the front
having been fitted by County
to indicate a one-man-operated
journey. In pursuit is another
'606', Yorkshire Woollen 57
(CHD 606), a 1958 AEC Regent V,
heading for Thornhill Edge on
service K (Dewsbury 'locals'
operated with letters rather than
numbers, Mexborough &
Swinton-style). Like several
other Tracky Tiger Cubs 594
would later be exported to the
Irish Republic, passing to a
County Kildare operator in 1971.
H. John Black

Unmistakably an ex-Mexborough & Swinton vehicle, 751
(CWY 319B) had been that company's first Daimler Fleetline when
delivered in 1964. It had only recently received Tracky livery
when photographed in Rotherham on a former M&S Rawmarsh
circular service, complete with informative M&S destination
blind. Later, having lost the characteristic moulding on the front
panel, it would serve at Barnsley as an Autopay vehicle. The site
of Rotherham's main bus terminal off Frederick Street managed
to look like an industrial wasteland, dominated by the cooling
towers and the gasworks, which were separated from the town
centre by the River Don. *Peter Yeomans*

At first NBC ownership seemed to make little difference, and until 1972 new vehicles generally followed BET practice, consisting entirely of Atlanteans, Fleetlines and Leopards in traditional red and cream. Well, almost! Four Willowbrook-bodied Atlanteans delivered in early 1969 illustrated perfectly the complexity of the early days of NBC: diverted from Devon General (and entering service in that operator's distinctive maroon and cream), they enabled Tracky to hire buses to Mexborough & Swinton, thereby releasing four Fleetlines for transfer to West Riding, which was struggling to cope with (or more likely without) its Wulfrunians!

Other new double-deckers delivered in 1969 were seven Atlanteans and seven Fleetlines with Northern Counties bodies, as in 1968. Thereafter most new vehicles until 1972 were single-deckers, including 50 Leopards with Marshall or Willowbrook bus bodies, 10 with dual-purpose Alexander Y-type bodywork and nine Plaxton coaches. There were also single-deck Fleetlines — three ordered by M&S and bodied by Marshall with high-backed seats and nine with Alexander bodywork to the dual-door layout then in fashion for urban one-man operation.

Early in 1969 a vehicle shortage arose but perhaps went unnoticed, as the Tiger Cubs borrowed from Trent to assist were also red and cream. Some were still with Tracky more than a year later.

The new deliveries saw many vehicles replaced, the last Leyland Royal Tigers and PD2s departing in 1969, while the first rebodied PS2s were withdrawn in 1970. Less welcome was the transfer in 1971 of three 1968 Leopards to the Calderdale Joint Omnibus Committee

After a spell in Devon General maroon and cream the Willowbrook-bodied Atlanteans received traditional Tracky colours. Having begun its journey exactly two hours earlier in Sheffield, 749 (RHE 449G) is seen leaving Dewsbury bus station on service 66 to Bradford. Despite its similar livery, the Leyland Leopard behind is not a Tracky vehicle but Yorkshire Woollen 249 (HHD 872), heading for Grange Moor on service 33. *H. John Black*

From the mid-1960s the majority of Tracky's coaches were bodied by Plaxton, the style evolving over the years. After various incarnations of Panorama came the Panorama Elite, which was introduced in 1968 and remained available until replaced by the Supreme in 1975. Tracky's first Elites were 118/9 (RHE 118/9G), 41-seaters on the short Leopard PSU4 chassis, which by the end of 1974 had been followed by eleven 36ft-long 49-seaters. No 118 was still in traditional livery when photographed leaving Doncaster North bus station, although NBC poppy red is visible on the double-decker in the background, showing Goldthorpe on its blind. *Richard Simons*

73

Mexborough & Swinton ordered three single-deck Fleetlines with 45-seat Marshall bodies for its White Rose Express operations between Mexborough and Leeds. However, by the time the services started M&S was no more, and because delivery was delayed the vehicles in question went straight into the Tracky fleet in May 1970 as 228-30. No 228 (THE 628H) was almost brand-new when seen at the bottom of Regent Street in Barnsley on 2 June, on a Leeds–Mexborough working of service X36. These vehicles were not a great success (why couldn't M&S have ordered Leopards like Tracky?) and after two years would be downgraded for normal bus work and renumbered accordingly. They were to survive until 1981. *M. A. Penn*

Single-deck deliveries for 1970 included 11 Willowbrook-bodied Leopard service buses (346-56) and nine Alexander-bodied Fleetlines (357-65). Leopard 349 (WHE 349J) is seen leaving Barnsley bus station on service 109 to Dewsbury via West Bretton and Midgley, with through fares to Bradford by connection. The 109 was introduced as a partial replacement for the long-established 66 from Sheffield to Bradford, which disappeared as part of a major multi-operator rationalisation in April 1971. *Peter Yeomans*

(a merger of the Halifax and Todmorden undertakings); Tracky was not used to losing good buses prematurely, and this was no doubt the result of an NBC edict. Remarkably one of the trio, 510 (NHE 10F), was still in service in Malta 37 years later — but that's another story!

In October 1969 Huddersfield Corporation acquired NBC's interests in the town's Joint Omnibus Committee but handed over the journeys to Dewsbury (services 26/27) and Sheffield (68) to Tracky. At the same time certain journeys on the 68 were extended through to Halifax — the first time a Tracky service had reached the town — and numbered X68. The Sheffield JOC was also wound up, at the end of 1969, the majority of its services passing to the city's transport department; the most visible impact for Tracky came in 1971 in the shape of five Park Royal-bodied Fleetlines which had been ordered by the JOC.

One of the high-points of the 1960s was the launch on 18 October 1969 of the 'White Rose Expressway' — a jointly operated network of fast inter-urban bus services using the M1, made possible by the extension of the motorway to Leeds in 1968. The original operators were Hebble, Sheffield JOC, Tracky, West Riding and Yorkshire Woollen. Services X31-X34 linked Sheffield with Bradford, Halifax and Leeds, while the X35/X36 ran from Mexborough to Leeds and were to have been operated by Mexborough & Swinton, using the single-deck Fleetlines. The services evolved over the years: in 1970 the Halifax service was dropped in favour of extra journeys to Bradford, while from 1975 the network embraced Wakefield. Leopard/Alexander Y types were Tracky's usual performers for the first few years.

In 1969 and 1970 the network changed little other than to absorb the former County and M&S services, but 1971 saw the most extensive revisions in more than 40 years. Huddersfield depot, in particular, was affected by NBC's need to rationalise, leading to joint operations with Yorkshire Woollen on services from Huddersfield to Bradford via Cleckheaton and to Leeds via Dewsbury or Heckmondwike — miles away from traditional Tracky territory and deep into the area which gave Yorkshire Woollen its name. Tracky also picked up an hourly service along the Calder Valley from Dewsbury to Elland and Rastrick, and this was later amended to run to the Old Raggalds Inn, way up on the moors between Queensbury and Denholme.

Since the County takeover Tracky had been running eight separate services between Barnsley and Huddersfield and now took the opportunity to simplify these while additionally taking on some journeys on West Riding's Wakefield–Holmfirth service. Elsewhere the long-standing joint services from Sheffield to Bradford (66) and Leeds (67) were dismantled, although the 65 from Sheffield to Barnsley was instead extended to Leeds via the old Burrows' route through Stanley. On top of all this the Manchester services were merged into one, running via Penistone and Holmfirth and then over Saddleworth Moor to Greenfield and Stalybridge so that, after more than 40 years, the Woodhead Pass ceased to be a Tracky bus route.

Barnsley town services were also revised, and 'Autopay' exact-fare double-deck one-man operation was introduced, first on the Athersley services and then, by the start of 1972, on several other Barnsley locals, including the old tram-replacement services to Worsbrough Bridge and Worsbrough Dale. The ex-M&S Rawmarsh circulars were also converted to Autopay.

Within three years of NBC's creation Yorkshire Traction's sphere of operation had expanded dramatically, but buses still wore the traditional red-and-cream livery, and the company was still very much the Tracky everyone knew and loved. However, further changes were afoot as NBC planned to eliminate local identities in all but name, and the last vehicles to enter service in traditional colours were Leopard coaches 26-8 (BHE 26-8K) in the spring of 1972. Thus drew to a close the 'glory days' — for now, at least — but this was far from being the end of the Tracky story.

At the time of its demise at the end of 1969 the Sheffield JOC had on order five Daimler Fleetlines with Park Royal bodywork, which appeared early in 1971 as Tracky's 752-6. These were the last double-deckers delivered in traditional livery, but even in Tracky red and cream they had an unmistakable Sheffield look. After a short spell on trunk services, during which an almost brand-new 753 (XHE 753J) is seen in Dewsbury bus station *en route* from Bradford to its intended home city on service 66, they were to lead uneventful lives as Autopay vehicles on Barnsley locals, surviving until 1984. *Peter Yeomans*

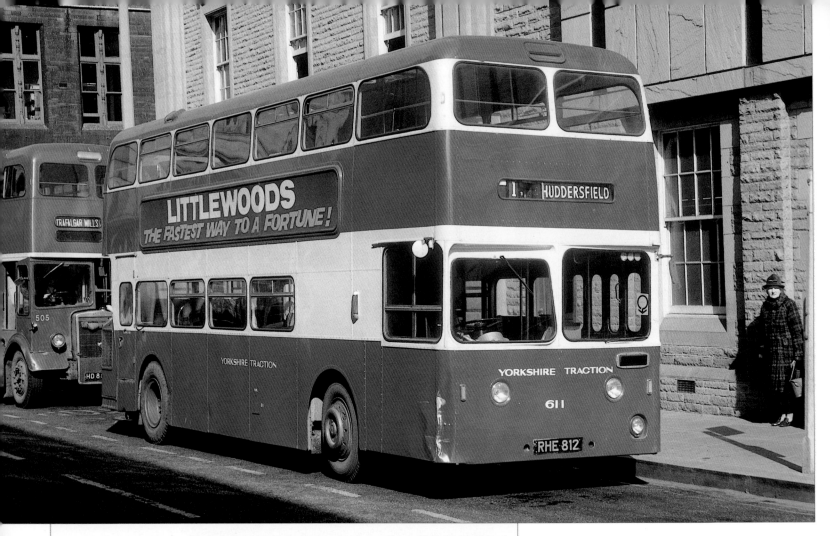

The lowbridge Atlanteans were not normally associated with Huddersfield depot, but 611 (RHE 812) had a short stint there, as this photograph reveals. Service 1, operated jointly by Tracky and Yorkshire Woollen, was created in August 1971 by combining the latter's service 1 (Leeds–Dewsbury) with the existing jointly operated Dewsbury–Huddersfield services. The Atlantean's traditional livery contrasts with that of YW's 505 (HD 8554), a Tiger PS2 rebodied by Roe in the 1960s, awaiting departure for Trafalgar Mills, in Leeds Road, Huddersfield.
H. John Black

New vehicles for 1972 included 25 Marshall-bodied Leopards — twelve 45-seaters and thirteen 53-seaters, the last of exactly 100 Leopard buses delivered from 1962. No 532 (CHE 532K), a short version, is seen here in Barnsley before working service 45 to Pontefract via Hemsworth and Ackworth, operated jointly with South Yorkshire Motors. These buses represented something of a watershed, being the last true Leylands before the Leyland National, the last underfloor-engined service buses and the last buses delivered in traditional red and cream. Very soon afterwards the 'glory days' would be over as NBC poppy red started to spread. In the background a 1959 Atlantean, now with a reduced blind aperture, is operating service 10A to Grimethorpe (White City). *Peter Yeomans*

Standing in Wombwell depot yard is Willowbrook-bodied Leopard 370 (CHE 302C), after rebuilding from express-coach format to a 53-seat one-man bus, retaining its narrow entrance. Previously it was numbered 208 and originally 1302; 1300 of the same batch had been exhibited by Willowbrook at the 1964 Commercial Motor Show. The photograph illustrates the stylised 'yt' fleetname which appeared briefly in 1971/2 —a late attempt to modernise the traditional BET-style image; a similar logo, but rather more contrived, would be adopted soon afterwards by South Yorkshire PTE. Wombwell depot closed in 2000, and housing now occupies the site which was once the 'car barns' of the Dearne District Light Railways. *Peter Yeomans*

9. NBC — the corporate image

From 1972 Yorkshire Traction lost much of its character. In that year NBC introduced the familiar white 'National' coach livery to help integrate and market a national network of long-distance services. Local buses did not need the same treatment, yet by the end of the year NBC had succumbed to the contemporary obsession with corporate identity and introduced highly standardised liveries for all its buses up and down the country: either 'poppy' red or 'leaf' green (or, during a brief period of indecision, blue). Given the stark choice, Tracky went for poppy red.

New buses from 1973 turned their back on tradition. For single-deck work the integrally constructed, rear-engined Leyland National was chosen (being, in fact, the only 'choice' NBC offered!), and 80 had arrived by 1979, 64 Mk 2s following by the end of 1982. As a staunch Leyland user, Tracky had never touched a Bristol, but ECW-bodied Bristol VRs became the new standard double-decker, some 106 having been delivered by the

end of 1981. The first National was 400 (FHE 400L), while the first VR was 800 (FHE 800L).

Leopards were still bought for coach and dual-purpose work. Here there was some variety, bodywork including Alexander, Duple, ECW, Plaxton and Willowbrook, while livery could be either white 'National' or red and white dual-purpose, vehicles switching from one to the other as circumstances dictated. Coaches bought under the 'New Bus Grant' scheme appeared regularly on bus services, reversing the position of the 1950s and '60s, when buses frequently deputised for coaches, and a white coach might turn up in Barnsley bus station even for the five-minute run to Rockingham Street, Tracky's shortest service.

Central Works' talent for rebuilding continued, and two of the 'new' Leopards used upgraded 1964 chassis, while 386 (EWB 386V) was a much-rebuilt 1965 bus with original Willowbrook body which Tracky managed to have classed as a new vehicle in 1979. Tracky was also a pioneer in re-engining Leopards, several

NBC poppy-red livery started to appear in 1972, and 21 (NWW 110E), being fitted for one-man operation for use on bus services, was an early recipient of the 'local coach' version. A Duple Commander-bodied Leopard, it was one of three such vehicles inherited from Mexborough & Swinton — the only ex-M&S single-deckers to last into the era of NBC liveries. This view in Rotherham bus station shows it operating from the erstwhile M&S depot at Rawmarsh on ex-M&S service 90 from Mexborough to Sheffield, which would later become the X90. No 21 was to have an exceptionally short life, being withdrawn in 1975 and sold for scrap. *Richard Simons*

acquiring DAF or turbocharged Leyland units for improved performance; despite their strengths Leopards struggled on hills, and it was somewhat embarrassing when the Bristol RE coach bought for a song by Ward Green Majorettes sailed effortlessly past an X32 toiling up a gradient on the M1!

Poppy red (which usually faded to a rather unpleasant pinky-orange) was also applied to older vehicles, including Tiger Cubs and Titans, and by 1977 traditional Tracky red-and-cream was but a memory. Vehicles still carried the Yorkshire Traction name, but individuality was suppressed, and, with the prevalence of Nationals and VRs, Tracky buses looked (and increasingly were) identical to buses labelled 'Cumberland' or 'East Kent'. These were emphatically not the 'glory days'!

Changes to local government in 1974 had a significant impact on the company's operations. The West Riding County Council was abolished, and the metropolitan counties of South and West Yorkshire were created, their Passenger Transport Executives taking over the local municipal bus operations (Doncaster,

Rotherham and Sheffield passing to South Yorkshire PTE, and Bradford, Calderdale, Huddersfield and Leeds to West Yorkshire). With the exception of the Manchester run (which, sadly, would be abandoned in 1981 in favour of a National Express coach service), all Tracky bus services ran within the two new counties. The PTEs handled network planning and set the fares; in theory Tracky merely acted as their agent in providing the services, but in practice company staff worked with them on service development.

Both PTEs adopted new yet surprisingly bland liveries — cream and brown for SYPTE and green and cream for WYPTE. After a time Tracky buses operating mainly in West Yorkshire received 'Metro National' logos, and several later appeared in full WYPTE livery. SYPTE went no further than requiring a discreet South Yorkshire County Council logo but made its mark in other ways, including the introduction of 'mobility' and 'Nipper' services in Barnsley, for which it provided Tracky with Leyland Nationals (equipped with wheelchair lifts) and Bristol LHSs.

Tracky's only dual-doorway buses were the Alexander-bodied single-deck Fleetlines (357-65) of 1970, which were originally to have had Willowbrook bodies, while three of them had been ordered by Mexborough & Swinton. They were withdrawn in 1981/2 after spending most of their careers at Rawmarsh depot. No 357 (WHE 357J) is seen in Wath Wood Road in 1980, working service 228 from Barnsley to Rotherham. This link was put in place only after the Mexborough & Swinton services had been merged with those of Tracky, and until the late 1960s passengers travelling from Wombwell or Wath to Rotherham had to change buses at 'The Woodman', about half a mile towards Rotherham from where this picture was taken.
John Law

Local authorities no longer dealt with vehicle registrations, and after 1974 few Tracky buses received traditional 'HE' registrations. The last registered under the old regime was VR 820 (SHE 820M); 821 had what looked like a Bradford registration (GAK 481N). However, 'HE' marks would continue to appear intermittently until 2001, when the system changed again, the last being X215 HHE on DAF single-decker 215.

As one of the more profitable NBC subsidiaries Tracky did not generally need second-hand vehicles. However, six 1967 Leopard coaches came from Ribble in 1978 and another from United in 1979, together with three Bristol LH coaches, not all of which were used. There were also two Leyland Nationals from Alder Valley and a refurbished former Plymouth Corporation example. New-vehicle orders often changed; for example in 1978 Tracky again ordered Atlanteans, but these never materialised, having been exchanged before delivery for more Nationals. There were occasional loans too, mainly to overcome vehicle shortages in the late 1970s: East Midland Leopards, Trent Atlanteans, Lincolnshire Bristol Lodekkas (which the trade union quickly blacked) and, best of all, bright-yellow Bournemouth Atlanteans.

Another acquisition was pure nostalgia: 492 (HE 6762), a 1935 Tiger TS7 rebodied postwar by Weymann and withdrawn in 1958, was bought in 1980 from a local preservation society and

restored to full PSV status. It has been used ever since for special occasions, including wedding hires, and even the odd guest appearance on bus services.

Two more long-established independents were taken over during the 1970s. Wray's of Hoyle Mill had worked the hourly Barnsley–South Elmsall–Pontefract service jointly with Tracky, mainly with second-hand double-deckers, since Taylor's (the other half of the Ideal partnership) had sold out in 1967. However, in 1974 Wray's too was acquired, while in 1978 Larratt Pepper sold its

Barnsley–Thurnscoe service, leaving South Yorkshire Road Transport as the last remaining independent running into Barnsley.

The PTEs indirectly funded investment in new buses, and after the VRs 73 ECW-bodied Leyland Olympians arrived in the years 1981-5. Instead of replacing the oldest vehicles some displaced six- or seven-year-old VRs to hard-up NBC subsidiaries in Lincolnshire and the South West — surely a questionable use of Yorkshire ratepayers' money. However, there were no more single-deckers after the last National 2s in 1982.

Typical NBC ECW-bodied Leyland Olympians were delivered from 1981, and 73 were in stock by the end of 1985. An early delivery to Shafton depot, 606 (OWG 606X) is seen at a notoriously tight yet famously photogenic spot in Hooton Pagnell, on the hourly 211 service from Barnsley to Doncaster via Grimethorpe and South Elmsall. Although in standard poppy-red livery the bus displays white WYPTE and NBC logos on the front panels and 'MetroBus' fleetnames on the sides, indicating use on West Yorkshire services; although just in South Yorkshire, Shafton depot ran many of its services 'across the border'. *Michael Fowler*

The nadir of NBC livery was the unrelieved all-red version, seen here on one of 64 almost identical National 2s delivered in the years 1980-2. With the steelworks in the Upper Don Valley as a backdrop, 220 (EDT 220V) climbs Nanny Hill in Stocksbridge, having operated from Barnsley via Penistone and Langsett on a short working of the 381 circular to Deepcar. The Stocksbridge by-pass now runs across the hillside of Hunshelf Bank in the background. *Author*

In the mid-1980s Tracky joined the trend of re-registering coaches to make them appear 'dateless'. Scrapyards and driveways were trawled for donor vehicles, which included BSA and Velocette motorcycles, Austin Cambridges and Volkswagen 'Beetles'. These often arrived on trailers at Upper Sheffield Road to satisfy 'the men from the Ministry' as to their authenticity before yielding their registrations. Original 'HE' marks were favoured, but a few 'YTCs' were also found; examples were HE 8899 and YTC 49.

The Conservative Party had regained power in 1979, and politics dominated events of the 1980s as never before. Much of what was happening locally was the very antithesis of Tory thinking, notably the legendary cheap-fares policy, funded from the rates in what by now was widely known as the 'People's Republic of South Yorkshire'. Nationalised industries were not favoured either (especially the National Coal Board, for which Tracky operated many contracts and specials until the bitter miners' strike, triggered in 1984 by the decision to close Cortonwood colliery, down the road from Wombwell depot). The most sweeping changes came in 1986, with the abolition of the metropolitan county councils with effect from 31 March, the first NBC privatisations in late summer, and deregulation of local bus services from 26 October.

The consequences for Tracky were enormous. From 6 April fares in South Yorkshire rose by a staggering 225%, the Barnsley–Sheffield fare increasing overnight from 25p to 80p, while the 5p fare for short journeys quadrupled. During the 'cheap fares' era loadings had to be seen to be believed, but it was inevitable that a huge loss of passengers would follow, and services were cut in May and July.

What better way to illustrate how Yorkshire Traction had lost control of its destiny than a green Tracky bus! By 1984 the company had largely been reduced to doing the PTEs' bidding as far as bus services were concerned, and WYPTE had started to insist that vehicles carry its 'MetroBus' livery. With a slightly jarring red fleetname across the front, Huddersfield-based VR 823 (GAK 483N) is seen in the town's bus station before operating service 218 to Leeds. Each PTE had established its own countywide route-numbering scheme, and Tracky was obliged to fall into line, bringing about some duplication of numbers — another Tracky 218 ran between Mexborough and Wath. Two years later deregulation was to change everything, and Tracky could reassert its individuality. *H. John Black*

More than 100 ECW-bodied Bristol VRs arrived between 1973 (Tracky's first ECW bodies since 1940) and 1981. Later buses, from 1978, were full-height versions, and several had scrapes with low bridges. After one such incident 924 (HWJ 924W) reappeared as a convertible open-topper. Not surprisingly there was little call for an open-topper around Barnsley, but it is seen here at Cawthorne in 1984 on one of its very rare topless outings for Tracky, operating service 236 in connection with an event at Cannon Hall. Later it was lent out to operate summer leisure services in Leeds and York, but after returning to Tracky its roof was kept firmly in place until privatisation and the acquisition of Lincolnshire Road Car led to a resumption of its topless career at Skegness. *Author*

Amid a sea of uniform poppy-red vehicles in Barnsley bus station, 1978 Bristol VR 864 (TDT 864S) stands out in its superbly executed replica 1930s livery; below the fleetname is the wording 'Established 1902'. The livery was applied in 1980 to promote the company's excursions and tours and features Scarborough, Skegness, and, a little more exotically, Boulogne. The bus was about to leave for Doncaster on service 223, invariably referred to by crews as a 'Donny-Mex'.
John Law

Well before bus deregulation, coach services had also been freed up, and National Express expanded in the early 1980s after the initial flurry of competitors largely disappeared. Upgraded 'Rapide' services were developed, and for the Barnsley–London service NBC provided two Dennis Falcons with Duple Goldliner bodies — Tracky's first Dennises since the Camplejohns' Lancet in 1961. What a contrast! They were put together hastily, at NBC's behest, and it showed: they were gone within a year. A return to Leylands followed, bringing Plaxton-bodied Tigers and Royal Tigers and a Roe-built Royal Tiger Doyen. Express coach travel was booming, and double-deckers were now needed; five MCW Metroliners were ordered in 1985 for the London 'Rapides', but instead came five Neoplans, with Plaxton bodies and 15.5-litre turbocharged Gardner engines. They were Tracky's first new vehicles on foreign chassis.

It was now 18 years since Norman Dean's retirement, and in the meantime there had been six General Managers. Frank Carter was next to take up the post, in February 1984, and, with circumstances about to change, his tenure would last more than

two decades, during which he had more scope to change the company than any of his predecessors.

For more than 10 years NBC had demanded rigid adherence to corporate liveries, but from the mid-1980s it allowed some relaxation, which gained momentum in the run-up to privatisation. Olympian 673 (C673 GET) was the final bus delivered in poppy red and also the last Leyland, ending a relationship that had lasted for more than 70 years. In 1986 a darker red was adopted, and in this livery came the last double-deckers delivered under NBC control, 16 MCW Metrobuses.

The main exceptions to corporate style were the overall-advertisement buses, often an unsightly mess of clashing colours, but several buses received special liveries to mark auspicious local occasions; a National 2 was painted in trolleybus-style Mexborough & Swinton colours as part of celebrations to mark Tracky's 80th anniversary in 1982, while an Olympian recreated County Motors livery for the Huddersfield transport centenary in 1983. Significantly, perhaps, Tracky did not mark the royal jubilees with specially painted buses.

The 'minibus revolution' was now in full swing, and one of NBC's final acts was to allocate 12 Mercedes-Benz van conversions, for which a use had to be found. They entered service on Deregulation day on new services based on Doncaster and South Elmsall, in a 'Townlink' livery of white, light blue and orange. 'D-day' saw many other changes and the predicted emergence of competition, notably from Pride of the Road (a name familiar from 1930s coaching, revived in 1981 when Wallace Arnold sold off its Royston depot), which started a service from Barnsley to Royston and Newstead.

At deregulation the PTEs were compelled to surrender their bus-operating role to 'arm's length' council-controlled companies, and Tracky could now run whatever services it wished without their say-so. However, the brave new deregulated world came as management attention was focussed on buying the company, and a cautious rather than expansionist approach was adopted. Within three months the sale was concluded, and on 28 January 1987 Tracky's NBC era drew to a close.

10. Independence

Following the buy-out Tracky was truly autonomous for the first time ever, raising hopes of a revival of the 'glory days' under local management. The deal included all the premises and 361 vehicles, the oldest (aside from 492) being Nationals and VRs dating from 1973 — not bad for £1.4 million!

The new image created in the final months of NBC spread quickly, but for Huddersfield and Rawmarsh depots the clock was turned back, and contemporary versions of County Motors and Mexborough & Swinton liveries were developed. There was also a red, white and yellow 'Fastlink' livery for Leopards, National 2s, Metrobuses and Olympians used on limited-stop services, including the new X22 to Leeds from Huddersfield and the X30 from Doncaster.

Minibuses were now embraced enthusiastically, and, of course, were cheap to operate. By the end of 1991 Tracky had bought more than 100 — mainly MCW Metroriders and Mercedes-Benz but also two Freight Rover Sherpas for a Metro contract and 10 Renaults (to be followed by used examples from London Buses). Many new commercial services were introduced, and contracts were won (and later lost) for services in unfamiliar territory around Elland, Holmfirth and Huddersfield. The Doncaster town-centre circular was also operated for a time.

Independence meant complete freedom in sourcing vehicles, and the reps soon came knocking. The single-deck coaches inherited from NBC were Leylands, but 10 Scanias were bought between 1987 and 1992, when the preference switched to Volvos; all were bodied by Plaxton. This combination was chosen for new coaches right to the end, the few exceptions being a Duple 425, two Scanias with Van Hool bodies and a Mercedes-Benz O404. Used coaches were also bought, including some final Tigers in the early 1990s, while others came from associated fleets, including a nice little Bristol LHS from Gash of Newark, DAFs when the coach operations of Jowitt, Tankersley, came into the fold, and a Bova from Road Car (as Lincolnshire now styled itself). From 1987 some coaches which were not tied to National Express or National Holidays work were given an attractive 'Coachlink' livery of deep red with gold relief.

The 'Rapide' double-deck fleet was strengthened by two MCW Metroliners and a Neoplan from other ex-NBC companies, and an MCW 400GT bought new; only three of these were built, and one of the others was later acquired second-hand. However, National Express soon reverted to specifying single-deckers for the London services.

The fact that Tracky's heartland was 'good bus territory' did not go unnoticed, and from 1989 there was an unrelenting series of competitive attacks on the lucrative Pontefract Road, Athersley and Kendray services. The newcomers came in all shapes and sizes but had no 'territory' of their own in which Tracky could strike back.

The competition was intense and sometimes aggressive, but eventually Tracky won through, and several operators' bus activities were bought out. Tom Jowitt Travel was first, in July 1990, forming the basis of a new Tracky subsidiary under the Barnsley & District title. At the opposite end of the spectrum Shearings, the Wigan-based coach-tour operator, decided to have a stab at bus operation in Barnsley (and in Tunbridge Wells, where the demographics were rather different!). A cross-town Athersley–Kendray service started in March 1990 and soon gained brand-new single-deckers; Shearings wanted a quality operation. However, within 18 months Shearings had new owners

The first version of Tracky's post-NBC livery retained the same layout, but a darker red replaced the 'poppy' shade, and the side fleetname was of a 'mock traditional' underlined style — without the NBC logo, of course. Rawmarsh-based Olympian 656 (A656 OCX) illustrates this at Pond Hill, adjacent to Pond Street bus station in Sheffield, then the terminus of service X90 from Mexborough — successor to the M&S 90. Note the Almex ticket machine; electronic ticket machines had yet to be introduced. *Author's collection; source unknown*

For a time coaches wore an attractive livery of deep red with gold lettering, seen on a 1979 Leyland Leopard with Plaxton Supreme IV body; the front grille was a Tracky modification to the original style. Keeping track of the coach fleet was notoriously difficult, and 17 (1737 HE), pictured setting off along Eldon Street past the Queen's Hotel to perform a school-bus duty, illustrates the point perfectly, being successively numbered 257, 157, 57, 17, 7 and 107; initially registered DAK 257V, it was to end its days with Tracky as GHE 696V! Issued originally to a 1963 VW 'Beetle', 1737 HE would later grace two Plaxton-bodied Tigers and a Volvo B10M. *Author's collection; source unknown*

who decided the bus market was not for them, so it packed up and left, selling Tracky eight Leyland Lynxes and the Wakefield Road premises. Possibly the most serious threat was gone.

A little later Pride of the Road was 'persuaded' to withdraw from Barnsley, having expanded since 1986 to become a major thorn in Tracky's side. Instead of taking on PotR's slightly dubious vehicles Tracky chose to acquire some Leyland Nationals with a more certain history from Northern General. Noting what had happened, local coach operator Globe immediately stepped up its competitive antics until its operation was similarly bought out three years later.

These were not the only competitors; SUT and, later, Sheffield Omnibus both ran between Barnsley and Sheffield, and SUT, successor to the original Sheffield United Tours, even challenged the X32 Sheffield–Barnsley–Leeds motorway express, using enormous Neoplan Skyliner double-deck coaches. It also competed within Sheffield but was bought out by South Yorkshire Transport (the former PTE bus operation), which passed on to Tracky 10 almost-new MCW Metroriders. Many others found the going tough and pulled out.

During these 'bus wars' many Tracky services came and went, including one in Derbyshire, between Chesterfield and New Whittington, introduced in a rather naïve act of retaliation against Sheffield Omnibus's incursion into Barnsley and operated by Rawmarsh depot. Sheffield Omnibus was also competing in Chesterfield, but Chesterfield Transport was not amused, and service 20 did not last long.

Well before buying out any competitors Tracky had bought the Lincolnshire Road Car Co (known for decades simply as 'Lincolnshire' but latterly as 'Road Car') under the NBC disposal programme. Shortly afterwards W. Gash & Sons of Newark was bought (and later absorbed by Road Car), Gash's Metroriders

joining the Tracky fleet. Over the coming years the Traction Group — as it became — expanded into Scotland, almost bought Darlington Transport and became embroiled in competition in Sheffield by acquiring a string of post-deregulation newcomers (Andrews in 1992, South Riding in 1994, Sheffield Omnibus and Yorkshire Terrier in 1995). However, these became separate companies within the group, independent of Yorkshire Traction, and their story will have to be told elsewhere.

Despite the group's move into Sheffield, Tracky largely avoided competing with Mainline (SYT's new name after an employee buy-out). However, Mainline had a role in backing a new competitor, Headlight, which appeared in 1995 and made life difficult for the next few years.

The competitive battles took their toll: costs were ruthlessly driven down, with a predictable effect on staff morale, revenue was depleted, fleet investment was reduced, and new opportunities were neglected. Worst of all, there was nothing new to show. Was this really what the architects of deregulation had envisaged?

▲ An attractive 'FastLink' livery, involving the use of yellow on a base of red and white was developed for limited-stop services. MCW Metrobus 704 (D704 NWG) additionally shows the revised style of fleetname as it leaves Wakefield bus station for Barnsley via Royston on the 446 — which was not a FastLink service. In the background a West Riding Leyland Lynx is visible in the bus station, while a Leyland National of competitor Yorkshire Travel waits in in Union Street. The Metrobus was Tracky's third double-decker to carry the number 704 ((the others having been a utility Guy and a LeylandTitan PD3) and by the time of the Stagecoach takeover had seen 19 years service. *Author's collection; source unknown*

▲ County Motors, 1990s-style. No 724 (BOK 24V) was one of five MCW Metrobuses bought from West Midlands Travel and painted into a 'retro' County livery with a fleetname of the style used for the main fleet. On 11 February 1992 it is seen outside the fine Victorian Kirkgate market in Leeds, working service 203 to Huddersfield via Dewsbury and Mirfield. Alongside is another West Midlands Travel cast-off, a Volvo-Ailsa of Black Prince of Morley, the renowned post-deregulation independent operator which was to sell out to FirstGroup in 2005, just a few months before Tracky succumbed to Stagecoach. *Author*

▶

By 1991 Tracky livery had evolved into this attractive style, which incorporated a blue band and was applied to all types of vehicle. Seen here leaving Hemsworth bus station on service 88 to Pontefract is 423 (L423 LET), a 1993 Dennis Dart with Wright Handybus bodywork.
Tracky had a total of 50 Darts (some of which were bought second-hand), including 20 Handybuses in 1992/3.
Tony Wilson

Many buses had appeared in the new County and M&S liveries, but from 1990 most vehicles reverted to standard colours, and in 1991 Tracky introduced a brighter livery, with red lower panels and white above, a thin blue band and a new-style fleetname in upper- and lower-case lettering. This was to be used for most of the next 15 years, also replacing the previous minibus colours and the red coach livery.

The notion of a standard Tracky bus simply did not exist in the privatised era. As with coaches, the first new full-size single-deckers were Scanias, five Alexander-bodied N113s arriving in 1991. By 1995 there were 25 Scanias, of three different models, including 10 bodied by Wrights (the very first Scanias bodied by this little-known Ulster concern, which had yet to hit the big time) and five each by Northern Counties and East Lancs (the first of many bodies from Blackburn). Dennis Darts were bought at the same time, with bodies by Plaxton, Wrights and Northern Counties,

including three nearly new examples from South Yorkshire Road Transport, following its takeover by the West Riding group.

Frank Carter's background was in bus engineering (he had served an apprenticeship with East Yorkshire), and he made known his liking for robust but simple technology. The Scanias were all very well, but they were sophisticated and expensive, and Carter's back-to-basics approach led him to import two US-built Cummins-engined Spartans for bodying by East Lancs; they entered service in 1996/7, the only Spartans ever to operate in the UK. The exercise was not repeated.

Rebodying was tried next. Yorkshire Terrier had six ex-British Airways Scanias with careworn bodywork, and the potential was obvious. East Lancs supplied the new bodies, but following rebodying two spent a few years with Barnsley & District before coming to Tracky. A similar exercise was carried out on a fire-damaged Scania coach acquired from West Riding.

Most eccentric of all was the KIRN Mogul, a Cummins-engined prototype built in Scissett by Keith Ward (whose company had manufactured Ward Dalesman chassis in the 1980s), with a view to setting up production in Poland to supply British Bus, but when that short-lived group sold out the project folded. Five years later Tracky 'discovered' the chassis and had it bodied by East Lancs; it took to the road in 2001.

Low-floor buses were *the* innovation of the 1990s, and Tracky's first were two Dennis Darts in 1997. These were followed in 1999/2000 by 25 Volvo B6s, another 10 coming later from Metropolitan Omnibus, a short-lived London operation in which the Traction Group had a stake. East Lancs were chosen to body all these vehicles having adopted a 'no frills' approach whichseemed to fit Tracky's ethos in its final years. Later single-deckers featured East Lancs bodywork on DAF and MAN chassis.

A vast array of mid-life vehicles was also bought, including Dennis Darts from Lothian, Optare MetroRiders from Trent, Scanias from Travel Dundee, Volvo B6s previously operated by Bebbs of Llantwit Fardre and Badgerline, and Volvo B10Bs and low-floor B6s from the Blazefield group. Older Tracky buses had regularly been passed down to other group companies, but now some came the other way, both from Barnsley & District and Yorkshire Terrier.

In the meantime the double-deck fleet was shrinking. Five MCW Metrobuses came from West Midlands Travel in 1990, and four Volvo Citybuses with East Lancs bodies arrived in 1993 when the group acquired the assets of Lincoln City Transport, but that was it for the 1990s. Not until 2002 did Tracky receive its first new double-deckers since privatisation — two East Lancs-bodied Volvo B7s, with lettering to mark the company's centenary.

The intake of new and used vehicles was not enough. The fleet had become ever older, with many NBC-era National 2s and Olympians remaining, and the 'Ministry' showed a close interest, resulting in the issue of various prohibition notices. A public

These pages simply cannot do justice to the multiplicity of vehicle types and liveries to be seen during Tracky's privatised years — certainly a return to the 'glory days' from the enthusiast's perspective. Popular vehicles which racked up huge mileages on the X32/X33 motorway services and the X19 between Barnsley and Doncaster were the ex-Lincoln City Transport Volvo Citybuses, extremely reliable workhorses with 80 high-backed seats. No 901 (E734 HFW — re-registered from its original KIB 6474) carries yellow Fastlink lettering on otherwise standard livery. It is pictured leaving Meadowhall Interchange for Sheffield city centre on service X32, having come from Leeds, and is followed by an Andrews Fleetline, also in Traction Group ownership by the time of this 1993 photograph. *Tony Wilson*

inquiry was held in 2000, and at a second inquiry in 2004 the Traffic Commissioner concluded that maintenance had fallen below acceptable standards and cut the company's vehicle authorisation from 350 to 250. This resulted in seriously dented pride rather than an enforced reduction in activity, but speculation about the future started to mount.

There were other signs that all was not well. To reduce costs Wombwell depot was closed in July 2000, the work being dispersed to other depots, but there was also a persistent staff shortage, and unreliability was a serious frustration to passengers. The company was not losing money, but profit margins were worryingly low.

Many services introduced during the minibus boom were withdrawn. Minibuses had got larger and more expensive, and latterly they had fallen from favour, although eight Mercedes-Benz Varios were bought in 1998, and Optare Solos followed later. Several longer inter-urban services were also cut back, partly as a result of improved rail services. Particularly notable was the disappearance of the once-prestigious White Rose Express services (early in 2008 only an hourly Rotherham–Barnsley service, maintained under contract to SYPTE, survives). Latterly Tracky ran the whole of the X32, and Arriva the X33; Bradford vanished from the Tracky network map, as later did Sheffield city centre, while Leeds was reached only from Huddersfield.

On a brighter note seven Scania N94 double-deckers arrived in 2004, mainly for the 226 between Barnsley and Thurnscoe, a long-standing service which closely followed the route of the old Dearne District Light Railways. They appeared in a startling livery of yellow and purple, destined to become standard for low-floor buses with both Tracky and Barnsley & District.

Following the humiliation of the Traffic Commissioner's ruling, 20 newer Olympians with Northern Counties bodies were bought from the Blazefield and Go-Ahead groups to help accelerate replacement of the last NBC examples. Oddly, they were painted red with a white band, mid-1980s style, as were some ex-Travel West Midlands Mk II Metrobuses acquired at about the same time.

Some of the Go-Ahead buses received 'HE' registrations transferred from coaches, while the Blazefield buses, which came from Keighley & District, sported 'YCL' registrations from their time on Yorkshire Coastliner's Scarborough services.

Eventually the inevitable happened, and it was announced on 15 December 2005 that Stagecoach had bought the Traction Group, with its 840 vehicles, for £26 million.

The period from 1987 may not have seen the hoped-for return to the 'glory days', but the company had been proudly independent for 18 years, an achievement in itself; only a few ex-NBC operators achieved great things, and most had been swallowed up by the new giants of the industry long before the same fate befell Tracky.

The final standard livery spawned many variants, with the development of subsidiary brands, usually with a 'link' theme; Economy Link (for low-fare 'competition bashers'), Dearne Valley Link, Rawmarsh Link and Easy Access Link were just a few. No 441 (P718 WFR) was one of Tracky's first low-floor buses, a pair of Dennis Dart SLFs with East Lancs Spryte bodywork, and had initially served as an East Lancs demonstrator. They were put to work on the Pogmoor/ Kingstone circulars in Barnsley, and 441 is seen heading over Jumble Lane level crossing, just outside the bus station, on service 344, the clockwise variant.
Tony Wilson

11. Barnsley & District revived

After Shearings' bus services were taken over Barnsley & District maintained the X10 from Barnsley to Sheffield via the motorway and Meadowhall, but the standard of comfort plummeted; whereas Shearings had used almost-new coaches, B&D provided elderly double-deckers or Leyland Nationals. No 826 (HWE 826N) was a 1975 VR transferred from Tracky (and destined to be transferred back again after B&D acquired some ex-West Midlands Fleetlines from the Andrews fleet). It is seen climbing through Worsbrough Park, past the entrance to the former Barrow Colliery, *en route* to Sheffield on 17 March 1992. *Author*

Tom Jowitt joined the post-deregulation fray in 1988, when he started operating between Barnsley and Hoyland, using ex-Scottish Bus Group Leyland Leopards in an unobtrusive livery of blue and grey. Other services soon followed, in direct competition with Tracky, using Leyland Nationals turned out in a bolder white, blue and red, and there was a move to a new base at Low Valley after the original premises at Pilley were outgrown. Tracky saw Jowitt as a particular threat and in 1990 made him an offer he didn't refuse; his fleet of 20-plus vehicles was acquired, including modern minibuses with wheelchair lifts used for contract work, and he brought his entrepreneurial flair to run it. The name was changed to Barnsley & District — maybe with a deliberate touch of irony. Jowitt's coach business continued independently for a time but also later passed to Tracky.

Following the takeover the livery was changed to a style which imitated Tracky's but with blue in place of red and with an additional red stripe, as well as a fleetname in matching style. When Tracky's livery changed again in 1991 B&D followed suit, but its version of the mainly white livery featured a blue roof.

B&D operated initially from Low Valley but relocated to the former Shearings premises in Barnsley after Shearings vacated them. The company functioned as Tracky's 'low-cost' unit, maintaining some of the ethos of the small but aggressive independent operator; it generally fell to B&D to tackle the competition around Barnsley and the Dearne Valley and to run any services retained from the acquired businesses, such as the ex-Shearings' X10 from Barnsley to Meadowhall and Sheffield. As such the company had no real network of its own.

If there was a heart to B&D's operation it was the 325 from Barnsley to Hoyland and Jump, which was built up to a high frequency to fend off potential competitors and even had new vehicles — three Alexander-bodied Volvo B6s, which for a time carried 'Hoyland Bus' fleetnames.

The original Leyland Nationals were mostly replaced by similar but newer vehicles transferred from Tracky, and these in turn by National 2s, while other Tracky cast-offs included Leopard coaches, MCW Metroriders and short-lived Bristol VRs. Other vehicles came from within the group, and the few double-deckers included ex-Andrews' Fleetlines, which had originated with West Midlands PTE, and Atlanteans from Sheffield Omnibus, which had begun life in the Eastbourne and Lancaster municipal fleets.

B&D expanded as the local bus interests of Shearings, Pride of the Road and Globe were acquired, this last deal bringing a mixed fleet of Nationals and minibuses. However, Tom Jowitt left and reappeared in the role of competitor, launching a vigorous assault against Tracky under the guise of Headlight and a string of associated companies. B&D now had to focus much of its attention on competing with its former manager, and services could change incredibly rapidly — some were deregistered even before they started, operating for just a few days! Jowitt was eventually forced to close down after various deals to provide backing fell through.

The later B&D fleet was more modern, with many used Volvo B6s and ex-Trent DAF/Optare Deltas, and towards the end there were no former Tracky vehicles left. The Hoyland services were upgraded by Volvo B10Bs acquired from Blazefield, which were painted in the new yellow and purple colours applied to low-floor buses.

Barnsley & District continued its separate existence until December 2005, when the Stagecoach takeover ended the 15-year reincarnation of Barnsley's original bus company, and in the summer of 2006 the remaining operations were transferred to Upper Sheffield Road.

12. Stagecoach

Northern Counties-bodied Volvo Olympian 608 (N418 JBV) had gained a Stagecoach fleetname and been renumbered 16868 by 24 July 2007, when it was photographed passing the entrance to South Yorkshire PTE's newly opened Barnsley Interchange *en route* to Darfield via Wombwell and Low Valley on service 69. Several used double-deckers acquired from 2004 were turned out in this reversion to late-1980s livery, and for a time this ex-London Central vehicle carried registration 2316 HE. The new interchange was built on the site of the original bus station of 1938, and a lengthy compulsory purchase battle was necessary to wrest it from Tracky's control. A century earlier, tramcars passed this very spot as they approached the town centre from Smithies. *Author*

From December 2005 Tracky and Barnsley & District became Stagecoach subsidiaries, trading as Stagecoach in Yorkshire (a title not previously used, although the group had toeholds in Yorkshire through the former municipal bus operations in Hull and Middlesbrough). Frank Carter left immediately.

Stagecoach changed very little until the competition authorities approved the takeover, but, with that hurdle cleared, 'rebranding' and investment gathered pace; by the summer of 2007 the Yorkshire Traction name had all but disappeared, and few vehicles remained in the old liveries — most had been repainted or replaced. Early casualties included the Metrobuses, which dated back to NBC days, and oddities such as the Spartans; the replacements included Leyland and Volvo Olympian double-deckers, Volvo B10Ms and new MANs. The survivors were renumbered in Stagecoach's national series early in 2006.

The inertia which had affected the Tracky network in its later days had to be tackled, and the biggest shake-up since deregulation took place on 20 May 2007, to coincide with the

opening of the new Barnsley Interchange. The changes were bold, and, whilst several new services were introduced, others disappeared after running for more than 80 years, including the one-time 11 from Barnsley to Doncaster via Grimethorpe, the former 27 to Rotherham via Wentworth and both long-standing Barnsley–Huddersfield services.

All the ex-Tracky depots remain in use, extending their long traditions of service to the local communities. Barnsley has been used continuously since the town's tramway opened in 1902, while Rawmarsh served as the Mexborough & Swinton tram depot from 1907 and was the second to notch up 100 years (Stagecoach marking the centenary by repainting a Dennis Dart to resemble a Mexborough & Swinton trolleybus). Doncaster and Huddersfield have been in use since the 1920s, while Shafton was used by Lancashire & Yorkshire before passing to Tracky in 1934. However, the Barnsley & District

premises in Wakefield Road were vacated in July 2006, when operations moved to Upper Sheffield Road. Central Works was also wound down, Stagecoach viewing it as an unnecessarily large overhead.

Despite the upheavals, operations in early 2008 are still technically maintained by the Yorkshire Traction Co Ltd and the Barnsley & District Traction Co Ltd, albeit with registered offices in Stockport. Continuity is provided at all locations by many long-serving former Yorkshire Traction staff, and Upper Sheffield Road continues as the nerve-centre, additionally now for the group's Sheffield and Chesterfield operations.

So, 105 years after its predecessor started running Barnsley's trams, Yorkshire Traction is still in business and, behind the identity of a major international public-transport group, continues to be the leading bus operator in Barnsley and the surrounding district. Long may it continue!

A magnificent reminder of the glory days is provided by 492 (HE 6762), the 1935 Leyland Tiger TS7 restored by Tracky in the early 1980s and still certified as a public-service vehicle (the '*Wedding Special*' lettering on the front indicating a useful source of private-hire income). The Weymann body dates from 1950 and replaced the Roe original, allowing 492 to continue in service until 1958, when it was sold via a dealer to an operator in Northumberland; it later passed to a showman before turning up at Central Motor Auctions in Rothwell, in 1974, and being acquired by a Barnsley preservation group. It returned to Tracky in 1980 and is seen here, aged 72, in the grounds of Chatsworth House, Derbyshire, on 24 June 2007. *Tony Wilson*

Bibliography

Yorkshire Traction — Early Development, by J. A. Sykes (Yorkshire Traction, 1982)
Yorkshire Traction fleet histories, Parts 1 and 2 (PSV Circle / Omnibus Society joint publications)

The Dearne District Light Railways, by A. S. Denton, FCIT (The Omnibus Society, 1980)
The History of the Mexborough & Swinton Traction Company, by C. T. Goode (published by the author, 1982)

Yorkshire Traction

TIMETABLE

WINTER 1965

PRICE **1/-**

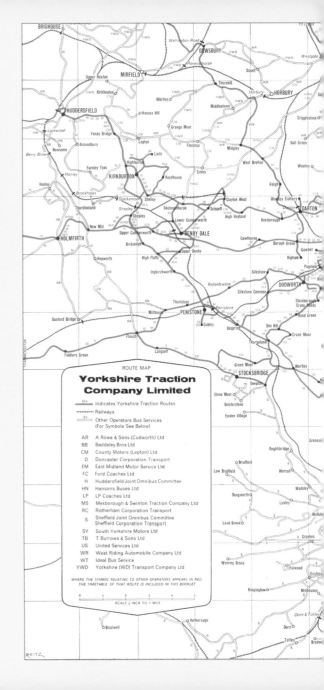

ROUTE MAP

Yorkshire Traction Company Limited

━━━ Indicates Yorkshire Traction Routes

┈┈┈ Railways

━━ Other Operators Bus Services
(For Symbols See Below)

AR	A Rowe & Sons (Cudworth) Ltd
BB	Baddeley Bros Ltd
CM	County Motors (Lepton) Ltd
D	Doncaster Corporation Transport
EM	East Midland Motor Service Ltd
FC	Ford Coaches Ltd
H	Huddersfield Joint Omnibus Committee
HN	Hansons Buses Ltd
LP	LP Coaches Ltd
MS	Mexborough & Swinton Traction Company Ltd
RC	Rotherham Corporation Transport
S	Sheffield Joint Omnibus Committee Sheffield Corporation Transport
SY	South Yorkshire Motors Ltd
TB	T Burrows & Sons Ltd
US	United Services Ltd
WR	West Riding Automobile Company Ltd
WT	Ideal Bus Service
YWD	Yorkshire (WD) Transport Company Ltd

WHERE THE SYMBOL RELATING TO OTHER OPERATORS APPEARS IN RED
THE TIMETABLE OF THAT ROUTE IS INCLUDED IN THIS BOOKLET

SCALE ½ INCH TO 1 MILE